TEXAS INSTRUMENTS

Graphing Calculator
Strategies

Middle School Math

TI-83/84 Plus Family
& TI-73 Explorer™

TI-84 Plus Silver Edition
TEXAS INSTRUMENTS

Author

Donna Erdman, M.Ed.

SHELL EDUCATION

Editor
Karie Feldner Gladis, M.S.Ed.

Assistant Editor
Torrey Maloof

Editorial Director
Emily R. Smith, M.A.Ed.

Editor-in-Chief
Sharon Coan, M.S.Ed.

Editorial Manager
Gisela Lee, M.A.

Creative Director
Lee Aucoin

Cover Designer
Amy Couch

Illustration Manager
Timothy J. Bradley

Imaging
Phil Garcia
Sandra Riley
Don Tran

Publisher
Corinne Burton, M.A.Ed.

Shell Education
5301 Oceanus Drive
Huntington Beach, CA 92649-1030
www.shelleducation.com
ISBN-978-1-4258-0026-0
© 2007 Shell Education
Reprinted, 2007
Made in U.S.A.

Table of Contents

Table of Contents *(cont.)*

Introduction

Introduction

Research Base

Teachers of mathematics have the dual challenge of managing the varying dynamics of their diverse classrooms as well as increasing student achievement across a wide range of mathematical concepts and skills. In the various mathematical subject areas, the TI Graphing Calculator can be an important tool that teachers introduce to their students in order to meet these challenges. With proper use, graphing calculators can meet the needs of all students by promoting higher levels of thinking, increasing student performance in math, and allowing access to mathematical exploration, experimentation, and enhancement of mathematical concepts (Waits and Pomerantz 1997). Graphing calculators were first introduced in 1986 by Casio and started a dynamic change in the way that mathematics was taught and learned (Waits and Demana 1998). As these tools improved and as researchers studied their effectiveness in mathematical instruction, well-known mathematical organizations, such as the National Council of Teachers of Mathematics (NCTM), have recommended that the appropriate types of calculators be used in math instruction from kindergarten through college (NCTM 2000). However, the tool will not achieve the lofty goals that educators have for student success all by itself. It is not enough to simply provide students with graphing calculators. Teachers need access to research-based effective strategies that they can employ for comprehensive mathematics instruction using the technology (NCTM 2003).

TI Graphing Calculator Strategies, Middle School Math and *TI Graphing Calculator Strategies, Algebra* are a set of books that offer the necessary foundation for teachers to translate simple calculator use into actual student comprehension of mathematical concepts, as well as the ability to perform mathematical skills. With the lessons provided in these books, teachers are given valuable techniques for integrating the TI Graphing Calculator into their instruction. In *TI Graphing Calculator Strategies, Middle School Math*, the students work on conceptual mathematical comprehension and then use the graphing calculators to further deepen understanding and retention of concepts in the areas of number sense, algebraic thinking, analyzing data, developing spatial reasoning, and working with units of measurement. *TI Graphing Calculator Strategies, Algebra* directs teacher instruction in maximizing student use of the graphing calculators while processing and learning algebraic concepts.

The lessons in both of these books are designed to give both new and veteran teachers the best strategies to employ. How well students understand mathematics, their ability to use it to work out problems, and their confidence and positive attitudes toward mathematics are all shaped by the quality of the teaching they encounter in school (NCTM 2005). Teachers no longer have to construct well-planned calculator lessons unaided. Besides lesson descriptions and materials lists, these two books offer step-by-step instructions for four key instructional phases: Explaining the Concept, Using the Calculator, Applying the Concept, and Extension Ideas. Each element has an easily identified icon, and when appropriate, the elements are combined for maximum learning of a particular math concept.

The TI Graphing Calculator Strategies lessons move students from concrete understanding of mathematical concepts through the abstract comprehension level, and finally to real-life application, while at the same time allowing students to develop graphing calculator skills. For teaching to be effective in a mathematics classroom, it is necessary to provide focused instruction that moves the student from the concrete to the abstract to the application of the concept (Marzano 2003). In the **Explaining the Concept** portion of each lesson, conceptual development is provided by integrating the use of manipulatives and hands-on activities before and during calculator use. Often with typical calculator instruction, the focus is purely on the procedure; however, research has shown that it is ineffective to emphasize a high degree of procedural proficiency without developing conceptual knowledge (Marzano 2003; Sutton and Krueger 2002). Graphing calculators can build on conceptual understanding by allowing students to practice numerous representations of concepts and experiences in a way that is not possible by paper and pencil alone. As a result of these methods, teachers are able to engage students more effectively by addressing different learning styles and developing understanding that leads to higher-level thinking. Teachers do not often associate the use of graphing calculators with the conceptual process. When students use concrete objects to represent mathematical ideas, they learn to organize their thinking and reflect on concrete representations (Florian and Dean 2001). The activities offered in the lessons engage students in building conceptual understanding while giving the practice necessary for procedural proficiency in calculator use.

In the **Using the Calculator** activities, students move toward abstract understanding. The lessons offer guidance in directing the students to practice using the calculator and improving their skill levels. Graphing calculators facilitate improvement in procedural fluency, the ability to compute, calculate, and use rules and formulas accurately with speed and confidence (Florian and Dean 2001). The **Applying the Concept** and **Extension Ideas** sections bring the students to the real-life applications and further practice. As students move through each phase of learning, they are exposed to a concept or skill numerous times. Per research, students should have multiple experiences with topics, allowing them to integrate the topics into their knowledge base (Marzano 2003). Overall, the challenging and interesting tasks found in application problems help teachers engage students in learning as they actively apply their knowledge (Seely 2004). As a result, students take ownership of new strategies and greater understanding of the ideas and concepts. Through the lesson extension ideas and the activity sheets, the students gain ample opportunities to practice. Students need to have extra time to process concepts and look at problems in different ways (Sutton and Krueger 2002).

Many teachers dread calculator use because of the classroom management issue; however, with proper use, calculators allow teachers to spend more time developing mathematical understanding, reasoning, number sense, and application (Waits and Pomerantz 1997). Therefore, these lessons help teachers respond to that concern by including an introduction with easy-to-follow tips for differentiating the lessons, grouping students, using manipulatives in the lessons, managing the calculators in the classroom, planning the integration of these lessons with standards-based curriculum, and using the graphing calculators in activity centers. The skills reinforced throughout *TI Graphing Calculator Strategies, Middle School Math* and *TI Graphing Calculator Strategies, Algebra* teach multiple representations of mathematical concepts so that students thrive in the mathematic classroom.

Correlation to Standards

The No Child Left Behind (NCLB) legislation mandates that all states adopt academic standards that identify the skills students will learn in kindergarten through grade 12. While many states had already adopted academic standards prior to NCLB, the legislation set requirements to ensure that the standards were detailed and comprehensive.

Standards are designed to focus instruction and guide adoption of curricula. Standards are statements that describe the criteria necessary for students to meet specific academic goals. They define the knowledge, skills, and content students should acquire at each level. Standards are also used to develop standardized tests to evaluate students' academic progress.

In many states today, teachers are required to demonstrate how their lessons meet state standards. State standards are used in the development of Shell Education products, so educators can be assured that they meet the academic requirements of each state.

How to Find Your State Correlations

Shell Education is committed to producing educational materials that are research and standards based. In this effort, all products are correlated to the academic standards of the 50 states, the District of Columbia, and the Department of Defense Dependent Schools. A correlation report customized for your state can be printed directly from the following website: **http://www.shelleducation.com**. If you require assistance in printing correlation reports, please contact Customer Service at 1-800-877-3450.

McREL Compendium

Shell Education uses the Mid-continent Research for Education and Learning (McREL) Compendium to create standards correlations. Each year, McREL analyzes state standards and revises the compendium. By following this procedure, they are able to produce a general compilation of national standards.

Each graphing calculator strategy used in this book is based on one or more McREL content standards. The chart on the following page shows the McREL standards that correlate to each lesson used in the book. To see a state-specific correlation, visit the Shell Education website at **http://www.shelleducation.com**.

Correlation to NCTM Standards

NCTM Standard Grades 6 – 8	Lesson Title and Page Number
Students will understand the meaning and effects of arithmetic operations with fractions, decimals, and integers.	*Order of Operations* (p. 31); *The Four Operations with Integers* (p. 54)
Students will work flexibly with fractions, decimals, and percents to solve problems.	*Making Sense of Percents* (p. 38)
Students will understand and use ratios and proportions to represent quantitative relationships.	*Solving Ratios and Proportions* (p. 46)
Students will develop an initial conceptual understanding of different uses of variables.	*Writing and Evaluating Algebraic Expressions* (p. 81)
Students will explore relationships between symbolic expressions and graphs of lines, paying particular attention to the meaning of intercept and slope.	*Using Patterns to Discover an Equation of a Line* (p. 67); *Representing Vertical & Horizontal Lines* (p. 74)
Students will use symbolic algebra to represent situations and to solve problems, especially those that involve linear relationships.	*Identifying the Point of Intersection* (p. 87)
Students will select, create, and use appropriate graphical representations of data, including histograms, box plots, and scatter plots.	*Creating Stem and Leaf Plots* (p. 95); *Constructing Box-and-Whisker Plots* (p. 111); *Making Circle Graphs* (p.119)
Students will use proportionality and a basic understanding of probability to make and test conjectures about the results of experiments and simulations.	*Experimenting with Probability* (p.103)
Students will precisely describe, classify, and understand relationships among types of two- and three-dimensional objects using their defining properties.	*Plotting Shapes on the Coordinate Plane* (p. 129)
Students will examine the congruence, similarity, and line of rotational symmetry of objects using transformations.	*Transforming Figures on the Coordinate Plane* (p.135)

Correlation to NCTM Standards *(cont.)*

NCTM Standard Grades 6 – 8	Lesson Title and Page Number
Students will use two-dimensional representations of three-dimensional objects to visualize and solve problems such as those involving surface area and volume.	Calculating Volume (p. 142)
Students will describe sizes, positions, and orientations of shapes under informal transformations such as flips, turns, slides, and scaling.	Tessellating with Regular & Irregular Shapes (p. 149)
Students will select and apply techniques and tools to accurately find length, area, volume, and angle measures to appropriate levels of precision.	Using the Pythagorean Theorem (p. 159)
Students will understand, select, and use units of appropriate size and type to measure angles, perimeter, area, surface area, and volume.	Computing Area and Perimeter (p. 167)
Students will solve problems involving scale factors, using ratio and proportion.	Constructing and Reading Scale Drawings (p. 174)
Students will use common benchmarks to select appropriate methods for estimating measurements.	Developing a Sense of Customary & Metric Units (p. 184)

How to Use This Book

TI Graphing Calculator Strategies, Middle School Math was created to provide teachers with strategies for integrating the TI Graphing Calculator into their instruction for common middle school math concepts. The lessons are designed to move students from the concrete through the abstract to real-life application, while developing students' graphing calculator skills and promoting their understanding of mathematical concepts.

The table below outlines the major components and purposes for each lesson.

Lesson Components
Lesson Description • Includes two objectives: the first is a mathematics standard and the second is a description of the concepts students will learn
Materials • Lists the activity sheets and templates included with each lesson • Lists additional resources needed, such as manipulatives and the family of TI Graphing Calculators
Explaining the Concept • Concrete instructional methods for promoting students' understanding of math concepts • Often incorporates manipulatives or graphing calculator technology
Using the Calculator • Step-by-step instructions related to the concepts in the lesson • Keystrokes and screen shots provide visual support • Often integrated with the Explaining the Concept section to promote student understanding through graphing calculator use

How to Use This Book *(cont.)*

Lesson Components *(cont.)*

Applying the Concept
- Instructional strategies to promote real-life problem solving and higher-level thinking
- Engaging activities designed around secondary students' interests

Extension Ideas
- Additional lesson ideas for practicing concepts and skills
- Can be used to review, extend, and challenge students' thinking

Activity Sheets
- Teacher- and student-friendly, with easy-to-follow directions
- Often requires students to explain their problem solving strategies and mathematical thinking

---

Icon Guide

To help identify the major instructional parts of each lesson, a corresponding icon has been placed in the margin. In some lessons, these four major instructional phases are independent; in others they are combined.

 Explaining the Concept

 Using the Calculator

 Applying the Concept

 Extension Ideas

How to Use This Book *(cont.)*

Integrating This Resource into Your Mathematics Curriculum

When planning instruction with this resource, it is important to look ahead at your instructional time line and daily lesson plans to see where *TI Graphing Calculator Strategies, Middle School Math* can best be integrated into your curriculum. As with most lessons that we teach, the majority of the planning takes place before the students arrive.

TI Graphing Calculator Strategies, Middle School Math is organized into the following five sections that are based on the NCTM strands of mathematics. Identify the strand or section of the book that relates to each objective or standard on your time line.

- Building Number Sense
- Analyzing Data
- Working with Units of Measurement

- Thinking Algebraically
- Developing Spatial Reasoning

The title of each lesson describes the concept taught with the graphing calculator strategies. Preview the lesson titles to find a lesson that correlates with the objective listed in your time line. The **Instructional Time Line** template (page 15) is provided to help integrate this resource into long-range planning.

Implementing the Lessons

After integrating this resource into your instructional time line, use the steps below to help you implement the lessons. The **Instructional Plan** template (page 16) is provided to help determine the resources and lessons to be used for the instructional phases: Explaining the Concept, Using the Calculator, Applying the Concept, Assessments, and Differentiation.

1. Familiarize yourself with the lesson plan. Make sure you have all the materials needed for the lesson.

2. Determine how you want to pace the selected lesson. Each of the lesson parts or instructional phases are mini-lessons that can be taught independently or together, depending on the amount of instructional time and the students' needs.
   - For example, you may choose to use the Explaining the Concept section in place of the lesson taught in the textbook or use the Using the Calculator and the Applying the Concept sections to supplement the textbook.
   - The lesson parts can be taught each day for two or three days, or the lesson can be modified and all three parts can be taught in the course of a 50- or 90-minute instructional block.

3. Solve the problems before class to become familiar with the features on the TI Graphing Calculator, as well as with the math concepts presented.

4. Because space is limited in lesson plan books, use a three-ring binder or a computer folder to keep detailed plans and activities for a specific concept together.

How to Use This Book *(cont.)*

Directions: In the first column, record the date or the days. In the second column, record the standards and/or objectives to be taught on that day. In the third and fourth columns, write the lesson resources to be used to teach that standard and the specific page numbers. In the fifth column, include any adaptations or notes regarding the lesson resources.

Instructional Time Line				
Date	Standards/ Objectives	Lesson Resources, e.g. *Graphing Calculator Strategies*, textbook, etc.	Pages	Adaptations or Notes

How to Use This Book (cont.)

Directions: Write the date(s) of the lesson in the first column. Write the standards and/or objectives to be taught in the second column. In the remaining columns, write the lesson resources and page numbers to be used for each phase of instruction, as well as any notes and plans for modifying the lessons or differentiating instruction.

Instructional Plan

Date	Standards/Objectives	Lesson Resources Per Instructional Phase				
		Explaining the Concept	Using the Calculator	Applying the Concept	Assessments	Adaptations/ Differentiation
		Pgs.	Pgs.	Pgs.	Pgs.	
		Pgs.	Pgs.	Pgs.	Pgs.	
		Pgs.	Pgs.	Pgs.	Pgs.	
		Pgs.	Pgs.	Pgs.	Pgs.	
		Pgs.	Pgs.	Pgs.	Pgs.	

How to Use This Book *(cont.)*

Differentiating Instruction

Students in today's classrooms have a diverse range of ability levels and needs. A teacher is expected to plan and implement instruction to accommodate English-Language Learners (ELL), gifted students, on-level, below-level, and above-level students. The lessons in this resource can be differentiated by their content (what is taught), process (how it is taught), and product (what is created). Below are some strategies that can be used to adapt the lessons in this resource to meet most students' needs. This is not an all-inclusive list and many of the strategies are interchangeable. It is important to implement strategies based on students' learning styles, readiness, and interests.

ELL/ Below-Level	On-Level	Above-Level/ Gifted
• Reduce the number of problems in a set • Write hints or strategies by specific problems • Simplify the text on activity sheets • Create *PowerPoint™* presentations of lessons and have students use them as a review or reference • Have students take notes • Use visual aids and actions to represent concepts and steps of a process • Act out problems • Model skills and problems in a step-by-step manner • Use manipulatives to explain concepts and allow students to use them to complete assignments • Have students work in homogenous or heterogenous groups • Have students draw pictures of how they solved the problems	• Have students take notes • Have students assist below-level students • Use activities centered around students' interests • Have students generate data • Engage students using *PowerPoint™*, games, and applets • Have students work in homogenous or heterogenous groups • Have students write explanations for how they solved the problems • Use the Extension Ideas to review concepts or skills	• Have students create how-to guides for functions on the graphing calculator • Have students use multi-media, such as the TI-SmartView™ or *PowerPoint™* to present how they solved the problems and/or used the graphing calculator • Have students work in homogenous groups • In addition to or in place of an activity sheet, assign the Extension Ideas • Have students take on the role of teacher or mentor • Have students create games for practicing concepts and skills

How to Use This Book *(cont.)*

Grouping Students

Recommendations for cooperative groups and independent work are given throughout the lessons in this resource. The table below lists the different types of groups, a description of each, and management tips for working with each.

Group Type	Description of Group	Management Tips
Heterogeneous Cooperative Groups	Three to six students with varied ability levels	Give each student a role that suits his or her strengths. Give each group a sheet with directions for the task and a description of each role in completing that task.
Homogeneous Cooperative Groups	Three to six students with similar ability levels	Give each student an equal role in the task by having each student take the lead in a different part or problem of each assignment.
Paired Learning	Two to three students with similar abilities or mixed abilities	When using manipulatives, have students sit side-by-side and give students an opportunity to manipulate the materials.
Independent Work	Students work individually to develop confidence in their abilities.	Closely monitor students' work to correct any misconceptions. This will help students retain the information. This is also a good time to work one-on-one with struggling students or gifted students.

Using Manipulatives

Many of the manipulatives needed for the lessons are templates located in Appendix C of this resource. Below are some tips for using manipulatives in the classroom.

- Use resealable bags or plastic bins to group the manipulatives together. Label manipulatives and place them on a shelf.
- If manipulatives are used for whole-group instruction, have a least one set of manipulatives for each student or for each pair of students. Create a transparency set of manipulatives for modeling on the overhead.
- Use labeled, colored pocket folders to keep activities with multiple components together. Store folders in cardboard storage boxes or sturdy plastic containers.
- Laminate games or instructions on how to use manipulatives to preserve them for multiple uses. Display charts and instructions on a bulletin board in the classroom.

Utilizing and Managing Graphing Calculators

Every minute of class time is valuable. To ensure that adequate time is spent on the lesson and on the usage of the graphing calculator, implement the steps below in your planning.

Methods for Teaching Graphing Calculator Skills

Unlike the four-function calculator, the TI Graphing Calculator has many keyboard zones that will be used to complete the activities in this resource. To help students feel comfortable using the TI Graphing Calculator, follow the steps below before starting a lesson.

1. Before beginning the lesson, demonstrate the most basic graphing calculator skills that students must know to be successful during the **Using the Calculator** section.

2. To teach a skill, have students locate the keys and functions on the calculator and familiarize students with the menus and screens these keys and functions access.

3. If multiple steps are needed to complete the activity, list the steps, on the board, or on the overhead for the students to use as a reference while working. Or use a projector to display the PDF versions of the Using the Calculator sections, which can be printed from the **Teacher Resource CD**.

4. Ask students who are familiar and comfortable using the graphing calculator to assist others. Let the other students know who those graphing calculator mentors are.

5. Allow time to address any questions the students may have after each step or before continuing on to the next part of the lesson.

Storing and Assigning Calculators

- Before using the graphing calculators with students, number each calculator by using a permanent marker or label.

- Assign each student, or pair of students, a calculator number. Since the students will be using the same calculator every time they are distributed, it will help keep track of any graphing calculators that may be damaged or lost.

- Store the calculators in a plastic shoebox or an over-the-door shoe rack. Number the pockets on the shoe rack with the same numbers as the graphing calculators.

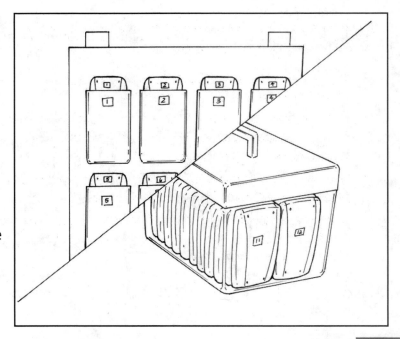

Utilizing and Managing Graphing Calculators *(cont.)*

Distributing Graphing Calculators

To distribute the calculators, consider at which point during the class period the students will need to use them.

- If the students will need the graphing calculators at the beginning of the class period, write "Get your calculator" on the chalkboard or overhead.
- If the calculators are stored in the plastic container, make sure they are in numerical order. This will help students find their calculators faster.
- If the calculators are stored in an over-the-door shoe rack, a note to take a calculator can be placed on the door. This way, the students can grab their calculators as they are walking into the classroom.
- If the calculators will not be used until later in the class period, have the students retrieve their calculators by rows.
- Once the students have their calculators, use the **Check-Off List** (page 21) to keep track of which calculators have been used during that day or class period.

Checking for Damage and Returning Calculators

After distributing the calculators, have students check their calculators for any damage.

- If a calculator is damaged, complete the **Damage Report** (page 22).
- When returning the calculators, have students return their calculators by rows.
- If the calculators are stored in a plastic shoebox, have them put the graphing calculators back in numerical order.
- If the calculators are stored in an over-the-door shoe rack, have the students place them in the correct pockets.
- DO NOT forget to count the calculators before students leave.

Utilizing and Managing Graphing Calculators *(cont.)*

Check-Off List

Student Names	Calculator Number	DATE					

Utilizing and Managing Graphing Calculators *(cont.)*

Damage Report				
Date	Calculator Number	Class Period	Damage	Reported By

Utilizing and Managing Graphing Calculators *(cont.)*

Facilitating a Calculator Center

If only a few calculators are available, create a calculator center in the back of the classroom. One suggested classroom layout is shown below. To prevent students from being distracted and to allow the teacher to work with the students in the center while monitoring the other students, have students sit in the calculator center with their backs toward the other students. Use the **Calculator Center Rotation Schedule** below to keep track of which students have been to the center. While working with the students in the center, provide the other students with independent work. Use the **Check-Off List** (page 21) to keep track of which students used the calculators.

Classroom Layout

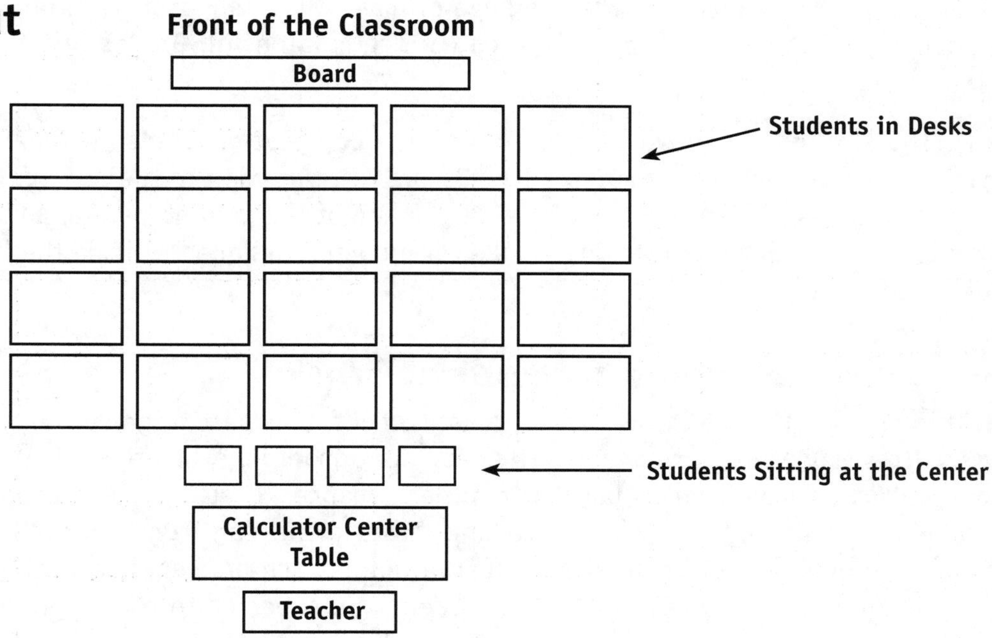

Front of the Classroom

Board

Students in Desks

Students Sitting at the Center

Calculator Center Table

Teacher

Calculator Center Rotation Schedule

Days of the Week & Date	Monday	Tuesday	Wednesday	Thursday	Friday
Group Names					
Students					

Assessment

For each lesson, activity sheets are provided that can be used to assess the students' knowledge of the concept. These activities could be considered practice, in which students' progress and understanding of the concept is monitored through an in-class assignment or homework. Or, they can be assigned as a formal assessment. For example, the *Practice! Practice!* activity sheets, are part of each lesson and can be assigned for homework, participation, or a completion grade. The activity sheets involving real-life application or problem solving can be used as a formally graded activity or assessment.

Completion Grades

To give a completion grade for an activity, have students exchange papers. Review the problems together. Model problems on the overhead or have students model the problems. Have students count the number of problems completed. Then use the **Completion Grades** template (page 25) to record students' scores.

Write students' names above each column on the **Completion Grades** template. Write the assignment title in the first column. Record students' scores as a fraction of the number of problems completed over the number of problems assigned. At the end of the grading period, add the number of problems completed for each student to the number of problems assigned. Divide the fraction to calculate a numerical grade.

Using a Point System for Formal Grades

When grading activities that serve as an assessment, it is best to grade them yourself. This provides you with an opportunity to analyze students' performances, evaluate students' errors, and reflect on how instruction may have influenced their performance. It also prevents student error in grading. Depending on a school's grading procedures, assessments can be graded with a fraction similar to completion grades. Determine the number of points each problem is worth. You may want to assign two or more points for each problem, if students are expected to show work or explain how they solved a problem. One point is awarded for the correct answer; the other points are for student's work and/ or written explanations. Write a fraction of the number of points a student earned out of the total number of points possible. Record these grades as fractions or convert them to percentages. Then enter them into your grade book or an online grading system.

Grading with a Rubric

A rubric is an alternative way to grade those activities or problems that involve multiple steps or tasks. It allows both the student and teacher to analyze a student's performance for the objectives of the task or assignment by giving the student a categorical score for each component. For example, if the students had the task of solving a problem and explaining how they solved it, a rubric would allow the teacher to identify in which subtasks students excelled or in which students could improve. The problem may be correct, but the explanation may be missing steps needed to solve the problem. The **General Rubric** (page 26) and the **Create Your Own Rubric** (page 27) can be adapted for various types of activities. By using an all-purpose rubric, students can also be individually assessed on specific skills and objectives.

Assessment *(cont.)*

Completion Grades

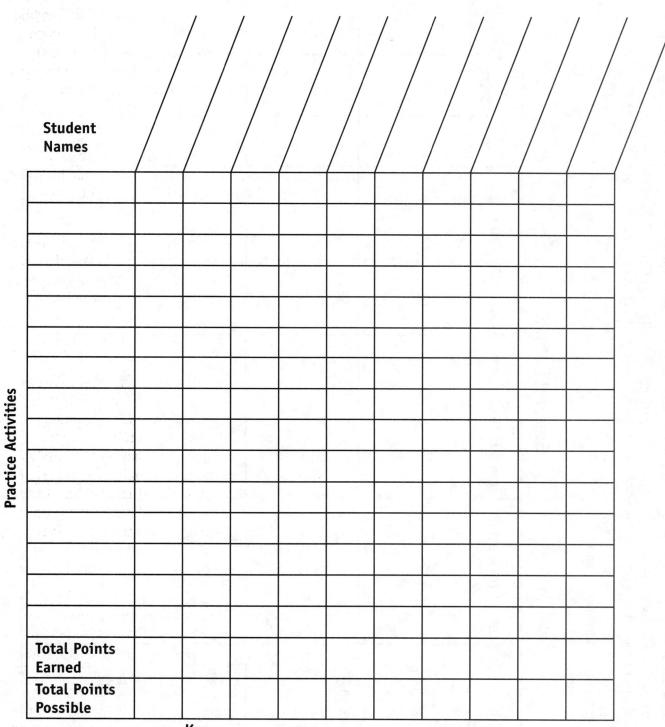

Student Names

Practice Activities

Total Points Earned									
Total Points Possible									

Key

Record Fractions for:
Number of Problems Completed
Number of Possible Problems

Assessment *(cont.)*

Directions: This rubric includes general criteria for grading multistep assignments that involve written explanations to questions. In each of the Level columns, specify each criterion by explaining how it relates to the activity and the levels of performance that can be achieved. Give the rubric to students for self-evaluation and peer evaluation. To evaluate an activity, circle a level of performance for each criterion and assign a number of points. Total the points and record them in one of the last three columns.

General Rubric

Criteria	Level I (0–4 points)	Level II (5–8 points)	Level III (9–10 points)	Self-Score	Peer Score	Teacher Score
Steps in the activity have been completed. Question(s) have been answered.						
Calculations are shown and/or explained.						
Responses relate to the questions being asked.						
Ideas are supported with logical reasoning and/or evidence.						

Assessment (cont.)

Directions: Write the criteria of the assignment in the first column. Then for each criterion, fill in the level of performance students may achieve. Give the rubric to the students for self-evaluation and peer evaluation. To evaluate an activity, circle a level of achievement for each criterion and then assign a number of points. Total the points and record them in one of the last three columns.

Create Your Own Rubric

Criteria	Level I (0–4 points)	Level II (5–8 points)	Level III (9–10 points)	Self-Score	Peer Score	Teacher Score

#50026—*Graphing Calculator Strategies, Middle School Math*

© *Shell Education*

Building Number Sense

Order of Operations
Building Number Sense

Lesson Description
- Students will solve addition, subtraction, multiplication, and division problems, including those arising in concrete situations, that use positive and negative integers and combinations of these operations.
- Students will use order of operations to solve a variety of problems.

Materials
- *Practice! Practice! Order of Operations* (page 35; nmbrs35.pdf)
- *Order Of Operations Challenge* (page 36; nmbrs36.pdf)
- *Cross-Number Puzzle* (page 37; nmbrs37.pdf)
- TI-83/84 Plus Family Graphing Calculator or TI-73 Explorer™

Explaining the Concept

Step 1   Ask the students the following questions:
- What are the steps for order of operations?
- Why is the order of operations important?

Step 2   List the following steps for order of operations on the board or overhead:
- **a.** Parentheses
- **b.** Exponents
- **c.** Multiplication and/or Division
- **d.** Addition and/or Subtraction

Step 3
- Model each step in the problem on the following page.
- To help students avoid using a number twice, have them cross out each step.
- Remind students to follow the steps of order of operations within parentheses.

Order of Operations *(cont.)*

Building Number Sense

Explaining the Concept *(cont.)*

Step 3
(cont.)

$8^2 + (-10 - 3 \times 2) \div 2$	
$8^2 + (-10 - 3 \times 2) \div 2$	follow order of operations within parentheses
$8^2 + (-10 - 16) \div 2$	
$8^2 - 16 \div 2$	evaluate the exponents
$64 - 16 \div 2$	divide
$64 - 8 = 56$	subtract

Step 4

Model each step of the following problem:
$-33 - 22 \div 2 + 9 - 8 \times 3 + 4^2$

- Remind students to cross out each step.
- Be sure to explain why it is important to evaluate the operations from left to right in the second, third, and fourth rows below.

$-33 - 22 \div 2 + 9 - 8 \times 3 + 4^2$	
$-33 - 22 \div 2 + 9 - 8 \times 3 + 4^2$	evaluate the exponents
$-33 - 22 \div 2 + 9 - 8 \times 3 + 16$	multiply and divide from left to right
$-33 - 11 + 9 - 24 + 16$	add and subtract from left to right
$-44 + 9 - 24 + 16$	add and subtract from left to right
$-35 - 24 + 16$	add and subtract from left to right
$-59 + 16 = -43$	add and subtract from left to right

Step 5

Have students work independently or with a partner to complete the first two problems on *Practice! Practice! Order of Operations* (page 35).

- Model each step of the problems on the board.
- If necessary, have student volunteers demonstrate additional problems.

Order of Operations *(cont.)*

Building Number Sense

Using the Calculator

Step 1   Use the problem, $8^2 + (-10 - 3 \times 2) \div 2$, to model how to solve a problem on the calculator.

- Have students input 8^2 by pressing [**8**] and then [**x^2**].
- Press the [**+**] key.

Step 2   Locate the negative key and parentheses keys on the calculator. Point out the difference between the negative key and subtraction key.

- Have students input $(-10 - 3 \times 2)$.
- Press [**(**]. Press [**(–)**] and then type **10**.
- Press [**–**]. Type **3**.
- Press [**×**]. Type **2**. Press [**)**].
- Have students input ÷ **2**. Press [**÷**]. Type **2**. Press [**ENTER**].

Step 3   To practice using the negative key, have students input the following problems:

     a. $-34 + 76$

     b. $55 - -22$

Step 4   To practice using the exponent key, have students input the following problems:

     c. 15^2

     d. 22^2

Step 5   To practice using parentheses, have students input the following problems:

     e. $(10 + 35) \div 5$

     f. $43 - (34 + 43)$

Step 6   Have students complete the problems on the activity sheet *Practice! Practice! Order of Operations* (page 35). Then, have the students use the calculator to check their answers.

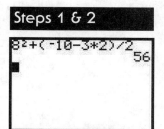

Steps 1 & 2

8²+(-10-3*2)/2
             56

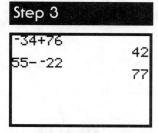

Step 3

-34+76
             42
55--22
             77

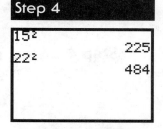

Step 4

15²
           225
22²
           484

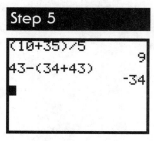

Step 5

(10+35)/5
            9
43-(34+43)
         -34

Order of Operations *(cont.)*

Building Number Sense

Applying the Concept

Step 1 Give the students a number, such as 45, and have students create two problems using order of operations to equal that number.

- Have students share their problems with the class.

Step 2 Give each student a different number and have each create a problem using order of operations.

- Give students guidelines, such as *the problem must take three steps to solve, and the problem must include exponents, parentheses, and/or integers.*

- Have students write their problems on a piece of paper. Use the problems as an activity sheet or daily warm-up activity.

Step 3 Have students create problems for the *Cross-Number Puzzle* (page 37).

- Then have students share their puzzles with classmates.

Step 4 Have students complete the activity sheet, *Order of Operations Challenge* (page 36).

Extension Ideas

- Have students use mental math to evaluate the following problems:

    a. 10 – 3 x 2 = 4

    b. 52 – 8 x 5 = *12*

    c. 35 ÷ 5 + 30 ÷ 10 = *9*

- On a separate piece of paper, have students write at least three word problems similar to those on *Practice! Practice! Order of Operations* (page 35). You may want to use the problems as an activity sheet or problem of the day.

Practice! Practice! Order Of Operations

Directions: Complete the following problems, then use the calculator to check your answers. Show your work in the space provided.

a. $3^2 + 6 \times (5 + -4) \div 3 - 7 =$

b. $9 + -25 \div (8 - 3) \times 2 + 6^2 =$

c. $150 \div (6 + 3 \times 8) - 5 =$

d. $-81 \div (5 + 2^2) - 63 =$

e. $3^2 - 4^2 + (13 - 4 \times 3 + 23) \div 4 =$

f. $(10 \div 2 - 12) + (-10 + 7 \times 10) =$

Directions: Write an arithmetic expression for each problem. Then evaluate the expression using the order of operations.

g. Mrs. Jones charged Bill $42 for parts and $12 per hour for labor to repair his bicycle. If she spends 2.5 hours repairing his bike, how much does Bill owe her?

h. A caterer charges a set-up fee of $45 plus $18 per person. How much will the caterer charge if 40 people attend the party, and the customer has a coupon for $75 off the total?

Name _____

Date _____

Order of Operations Challenge

Directions: Complete the following problems, then use the calculator to check your answers. Show your work in the space provided.

a. $\dfrac{(11 - 3 \times 4) + (8 + 54 \div -3)}{4 + 5 \times 8 - 33 \div 11 - 14} =$

b. $\dfrac{8^2 + (150 - 168 + 14) - 5^2}{3 \times 11 - 15 \div 3 + 70 \div 10} =$

c. $\dfrac{86 - 43 + 12 \times 4 - 33}{65 + 15 \times 5 - 207 \div 3} =$

d. $\dfrac{4^2 + 6 \times 3 - 54 \div 9}{6^2 - (57 - 4 \times 8)}$ **+** $\dfrac{(30 \times 5 - 12 \times 5) + 3 - 72}{55 - (37 + 28 \div 4)} =$

Cross-Number Puzzle

Directions: Use the calculator to create ten order of operations problems with solutions that fit the boxes in the number puzzle. Record the problems in the clue lines below the puzzle.

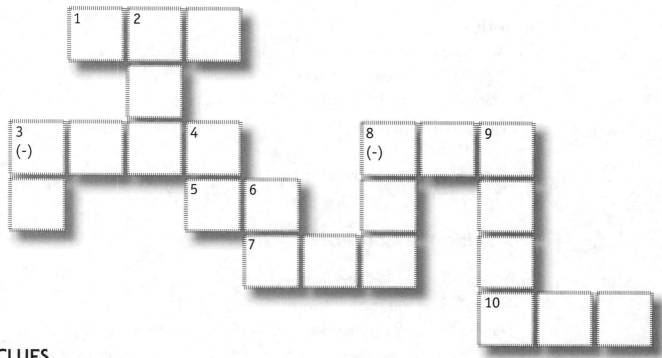

CLUES

Across

1. _____

3. (-) _____

5. _____

7. _____

8. (-) _____

10. _____

Down

2. _____

3. (-) _____

4. _____

6. _____

8. (-) _____

9. _____

Making Sense of Percents

Building Number Sense

Lesson Description

- Students will convert fractions, decimals, and percents and will use these equivalent forms in estimations, calculations, and applications.
- Students will calculate the percent of a number to solve a variety of problems.

Materials

- **Appendix C**: *Decimal Squares* (page 199; appnd199.pdf)
- Transparency of *Decimal Squares*
- *Practice! Practice! Percents* (page 42; nmbrs42.pdf)
- *Fractions, Decimals, & Percents* (page 43; nmbrs43.pdf)
- *Final Grade* (page 44; nmbrs44.pdf)
- *Grade Sheet* (page 45; nmbrs45.pdf)
- TI-83/84 Plus Family Graphing Calculator or TI-73 Explorer™

Explaining the Concept

Step 1   Ask the students the following questions:

- What does *percent* mean? *Answer: Per hundred*
- How many places behind the decimal is the hundredths place? *Answer: Two*
- How do you change a percent to a decimal? *Answer: Move the decimal two places to the left.*
- How do you change a decimal to a percent? *Answer: Move the decimal two places to the right.*

Step 2   Give each student a copy of *Decimal Squares* (page 199) and place a transparency of *Decimal Squares* on the overhead.

- Ask students how many units each square is divided into. Ask students what is the area of each square. *Answer: One Hundred*
- Have students explain how they determined their answers.

Explaining the Concept (cont.)

Step 3
Write 30%, 30/100, and 0.30 on the overhead. Ask students if the three numbers listed represent equivalent values. *Answer: Yes*

- Use a decimal square to show that all three values are equivalent. Have the students shade an area of 30 units and then explain that the fraction for the shaded area is 30/100 because 30 out of 100 units are shaded.

- Explain that the percent is 30% because the definition of percent is per hundred, and the decimal is 0.30 because the hundredths place is two places behind the decimal.

Step 4
Have students shade in 65 units and as a class write the fraction, decimal, and percent for the shaded area. *Answer: 65/100, .65, 65%*

- Model for students how to change a decimal to a percent. *(Move the decimal two places to the right and add a percent sign, or multiply by 100.)*

- Model how to change a percent to a decimal. *(Drop the percent sign and move the decimal two places to the left, or divide by 100.)*

Step 5
Have students shade in the units listed below and write the fraction, decimal, and percent for each shaded area. Then discuss their answers.

- **a.** 65 units *Answer: 67/100, .67, 67%*
- **b.** 8 units *Answer: 8/100, .08, 8%*
- **c.** 44 1/2 units *Answer: 44.5/100, .445, 44.5%*
- **d.** 125 units *Answer: 125/100, 1.25, 125%*

Step 6
Draw 14 dots on the board or overhead and ask students, "What number is 50% of 14?" *Answer: Seven*

- Explain to students that 50% is equivalent to 1/2, which means one out of two. Draw two boxes on the board and divide the 14 dots between the two boxes.

Making Sense of Percents *(cont.)*

Building Number Sense

Explaining the Concept *(cont.)*

Step 7

Explain that 50% of 14, can be written as a multiplication problem because the word "of" means to multiply.

- Explain that before multiplying, 50% must first be changed to a fraction or decimal. *Answer: 50/100, .50*
- Solve the problem by using both a fraction and decimal. *Answer: 7*

Step 8

Have students work with a partner to complete the activity sheet, *Practice! Practice! Percents* (page 42).

- Allow students to use decimal squares to aid their conceptual understanding.

Using the Calculator

Step 1

Using the problem "What number is 50% of 14?" model how to calculate the problem on the graphing calculator.

- First, have students change % into a decimal by either moving the decimal point or dividing by 100.
- Have students input 0.50 into the graphing calculator.
- Model how to use the decimal key. Press [·] and then type **50**.
- Press the multiplication key [×] and then type **14**. Press [ENTER].

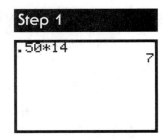

Step 2

Working together, use the graphing calculator to solve the following problems.

- **a.** 73% of 115 = *83.95*
- **b.** 12% of 345 = *41.4*
- **c.** 5% of 46 = *2.3*
- **d.** 45.5% of 105 = *47.775*
- **e.** 145% of 60 = *87*

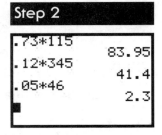

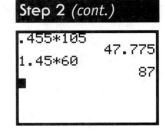

Making Sense of Percents *(cont.)*

Building Number Sense

Applying the Concept

Step 1   Brainstorm a list with students of real-life situations that involve percents.

- Discuss with students the most common fractions found in real-life situations.

Step 2   Then have students complete the activity sheet *Fractions, Decimals, & Percents* (page 43) to practice finding the equivalent forms of the most common fractions.

Step 3   Model the first problem on the activity sheet, *Final Grade* (page 44).

- Explain to students that some types of activities, such as tests and quizzes, are given more weight in a final grade than others. These weighted grades are represented by a percentage of the final grade.
- Ask students, "What is the sum of the weighted percentages for a class?" Answer: 100

Step 4   Ask students what mathematical operations and steps they would use to calculate their final grades, if they knew the percentage weights for their tests, quizzes, homework, and projects.

- *Answer: Average the grades together for each weighted category. Convert the weighted percent to a decimal and multiply it by the average. Then find the sum of the weighted percentages.*

Step 5   Have students complete the remaining problems on the *Final Grade* activity sheet (page 44).

Step 6   Using the *Grade Sheet* (page 45), have students record their grades and then calculate their final grades at the end of the grading period.

Extension Ideas

- Have students keep track of their grades in another class and then calculate their final grades at the end of the grading period.
- To enhance mental math skills, have students evaluate problems such as 50% of 120, 25% of 32, or 75% of 100.
- Have students practice memorizing the most common fractions on the activity sheet, *Fractions, Decimals, & Percents* (page 43).

Name _____

Date _____

Practice! Practice! Percents

Directions: Change the percents to decimals.

a. 17% = _____

b. 177% = _____

c. $25\frac{1}{2}$% = _____

d. 3% = _____

Directions: Change the percents to decimals, then use your graphing calculator to solve the problems.

e. What is 49% of 792?

f. What is 2% of 66?

g. What is $49\frac{1}{2}$ of 505?

h. What is 175% of 222?

i. What is 32.5% of 155?

j. What is 112% of 433?

k. What is 15.7% of 43?

l. What is 21% of 654?

m. What is 9% of 123?

n. What is 4% of 44?

Name _____

Date _____

Fractions, Decimals, & Percents

Directions: Change the fractions to decimals and percents. Round the decimals to the nearest hundredth.

Fraction	Decimal	Percent
$\frac{1}{3}$		
$\frac{2}{3}$		
$\frac{1}{4}$		
$\frac{2}{4}$		
$\frac{3}{4}$		
$\frac{1}{5}$		
$\frac{2}{5}$		
$\frac{3}{5}$		
$\frac{4}{5}$		
$\frac{1}{6}$		

Fraction	Decimal	Percent
$\frac{2}{6}$		
$\frac{3}{6}$		
$\frac{4}{6}$		
$\frac{5}{6}$		
$\frac{1}{8}$		
$\frac{2}{8}$		
$\frac{3}{8}$		
$\frac{4}{8}$		
$\frac{5}{8}$		
$\frac{6}{8}$		
$\frac{7}{8}$		

Final Grade

Directions: Allison wants to calculate her grade in each of her classes. The grading scale below is used by all of the teachers at her school, but each of Allison's teachers calculates her grade differently. Using the information in each problem, help Allison determine her grade in each class. Show your work on a separate piece of paper.

A	94–100
B	85–93
C	75–84
D	65–74

a. In English, Allison's writing assignment grades were 79, 96, 83, 72, 88, and 75. Her vocabulary quiz scores were 89, 45, 69, 72, 83, and 77. She received a 94, 88, and 99 on her book reports. Her test grades were 87 and 76. Allison's English teacher counts the writing assignment average as 40% of the final grade, the unit test average as 30% of the final grade, the vocabulary quiz average as 20% of the final grade, and the book report average as 10% of the final grade.

   What is her average?_____   **What is her letter grade?**_____

b. In math, Allison had quiz grades of 78, 89, 64, 88, 93, and 75. Her chapter test grades were 89, 91, and 85. Her project grade was 94. Allison's math teacher counts each quiz grade as 5% of her final grade, the project as 10%, and the chapter test average as 60% of her final grade.

   What is her average? _____   **What is her letter grade?**_____

c. In science, Allison's lab grades were 92, 94, 88, 74, and 77. Her test grades were 92, 85, and 78. Her project grade was 83. The science teacher counts the test average as 55% of the final grade, the lab average as 40% of the final grade, and the project as 5% of the final grade.

   What is her average? _____   **What is her letter grade?** _____

d. Allison's history teacher counts the quiz average as 15% of the final grade, the projects average as 20%, and the test average as 65%. Allison's quiz grades were 65, 77, 72, and 81. Her test grades were 80 and 84. Her project grades were 89 and 81.

   What is her average? _____   **What is her letter grade?** _____

Name

Date

Grade Sheet

Directions: Use the table below to determine your final grade in the class. In the first row, fill in the percentage of the final grade for tests, quizzes, homework, and projects. Then record your grades in the appropriate columns. Average the grades together and calculate the percentage of the average. Calculate your final grade at the end of the grading period.

____% of final grade	____% of final grade	____% of final grade	____% of final grade
Test Grades	**Quiz Grades**	**Homework Grades**	**Project Grades**
% of average =	**% of average =**	**% of average =**	**% of average =**

My final grade is: _____

On the lines below, explain how you calculated the final grade.

_____

_____

_____

Solving Ratios & Proportions

Building Number Sense

Lesson Description

- Students will use cross-multiplication to solve proportion problems, understanding the process as the multiplication of both sides of an equation by a multiplicative inverse.
- Students will use proportions to solve a variety of problems.

Materials

- *Practice! Practice! Ratios & Proportions* (page 49; nmbrs49.pdf)
- *Jambalaya Proportions* (pages 50–51; nmbrs50.pdf)
- *Applying Ratios & Proportions* (page 52; nmbrs52.pdf)
- *How Many Fish? Hands-On Activity* (page 53; nmbrs53.pdf)
- TI-83/84 Plus Family Graphing Calculator or TI-73 Explorer™

Explaining the Concept/Using the Calculator

Step 1

Ask students the following questions:

- What is a ratio? *Answer: A ratio is a comparison of two numbers using division.*
- What is a proportion? *Answer: An equation showing that two ratios are equivalent.*

Step 2

Give students a handful of colored beads, buttons, or attribute blocks. Have students write at least 6 ratios describing the attributes of the objects.

- Have the students share their ratios with the class. Examples may include: red beads to yellow beads and small buttons to large buttons.

Step 3

Using a ratio, ask students to double the ratio.

- Write both ratios on the board or overhead. Ask students if the two ratios are equal. *Answer: Yes.* Place an equal sign between the two ratios.
- Explain to students that two equal ratios are called a proportion.

Step 4

Using another ratio, triple one part of the ratio and leave the other as an unknown.

- Ask students to give the value for the unknown.
- Cross multiply the proportion to show that the two ratios are equal.

Solving Ratios & Proportions *(cont.)*

Building Number Sense

Explaining the Concept/Using the Calculator *(cont.)*

Step 5

Use problem **a** on the activity sheet, *Practice! Practice! Ratios* and *Proportions (page 49)*, to model how to cross-multiply to solve for the unknown.

$$\frac{56}{70} = \frac{672}{x}$$

$$56x = 70 \cdot 672$$

Step 6

After students cross multiply with the variable, explain how to calculate the product of the other two values on the graphing calculator.

- Press ⌜7⌝ ⌜0⌝ to input the first value. Press ✖ to input the multiplication sign.

- Press ⌜6⌝ ⌜7⌝ ⌜2⌝ to input the second value. Press **ENTER** to evaluate the expression.

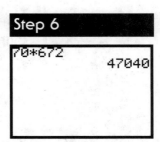

Step 7

Show students how to write the products as an equation and then solve for the unknown.

$$56x = 47,040$$

$$47,040 \div 56$$

$$x = 840$$

- Press ⌜4⌝ ⌜7⌝ ⌜0⌝ ⌜4⌝ ⌜0⌝ to input the dividend. Press ➗ to input the operation.

- Press ⌜5⌝ ⌜6⌝ to input the divisor. Press **ENTER** to execute the operation.

Step 8

Have students complete the activity sheet, *Practice! Practice! Ratios & Proportions* (page 49). Review the problems with the students.

Solving Ratios & Proportions *(cont.)*

Building Number Sense

Applying the Concept

Step 1   On the board or overhead, write a recipe containing five or fewer ingredients and the number of servings it makes.

Step 2   Ask students to explain how to write a proportion for each ingredient to feed the entire class.

Step 3   Using the graphing calculator, have students calculate the amount needed for each ingredient to serve the entire class.

Step 4   Review the example on the activity sheet, *Jambalaya Proportions* (pages 50–51). Have students complete the activity sheet. Review the problems with the students.

Step 5   Have students complete the activity sheet, *Applying Ratios & Proportions* (page 52). Review the problems with the students.

Extension Ideas

- To enhance mental math skills, give students a ratio such as 5/6 and ask them to double the ratio.
- Use the *How Many Fish? Hands-On Activity* (page 53) to help students understand ratios and proportions more concretely.

Practice! Practice! Ratios and Proportions

Directions: Solve. Show your work in the space provided.

a. $\dfrac{56}{70} = \dfrac{672}{x}$

f. $\dfrac{x}{800} = \dfrac{15}{32}$

b. $\dfrac{13}{21} = \dfrac{x}{189}$

g. $\dfrac{176}{x} = \dfrac{16}{25}$

c. $\dfrac{x}{85} = \dfrac{21}{34}$

h. $\dfrac{16}{17} = \dfrac{120}{x}$

d. $\dfrac{14}{23} = \dfrac{x}{74.75}$

i. $\dfrac{94}{x} = \dfrac{8}{11}$

e. $\dfrac{x}{37.125} = \dfrac{6}{9}$

j. $\dfrac{25}{35} = \dfrac{165}{x}$

Name _____

Date _____

Jambalaya Proportions

Directions: Convert each fraction in the recipe to a decimal. DO NOT ROUND. Record the decimal equivalent to the left of the ingredient on the table. Using a proportion, calculate the amount of ingredients needed for 8 servings and for 2 servings. The example below shows the number of green peppers needed for four servings.

$$\frac{1}{4} \text{ cup chopped green pepper } = \frac{0.25}{4} = \frac{x}{2} \qquad x = 0.125$$

Maw Maw's Famous Jambalaya (Serves 4)

$\frac{1}{2}$ cup chopped green onion $1\frac{1}{2}$ cups sausage

$\frac{3}{4}$ cup chopped white onion $1\frac{3}{4}$ lb. chicken

$\frac{1}{4}$ cup chopped green pepper $2\frac{1}{2}$ cups diced tomatoes

$\frac{1}{8}$ cup chopped celery $1\frac{1}{4}$ cups water

2 teaspoons crushed garlic   1 cup raw rice

$\frac{3}{8}$ cup melted butter

Jambalaya Proportions *(cont.)*

Using the Calculator

To find the decimal and fraction equivalent for each ingredient, convert the decimal to a fraction. Follow the steps below to convert 0.125 to a fraction.

- Type the number and then press **MATH** to access the Math menu.

- Press **ENTER** to paste the Frac command on the Home screen, and press **ENTER** to execute the command.

4 Servings		8 Servings		2 Servings	
Decimal	**Ingredients**	**Decimal**	**Fraction**	**Decimal**	**Fraction**
	green onion				
	white onion				
	green pepper				
	celery				
	garlic				
	butter				
	sausage				
	chicken				
	tomatoes				
	water				
	rice				

Name _____

Date _____

Applying Ratios and Proportions

Directions: Solve by using a proportion. Show your work in the space provided.

a. The directions on the bag of cement state to mix every 4 buckets of cement with 2 buckets of water. Mr. Jones has 10 buckets of cement mix; how many buckets of water does he need?

b. A seventh-grade class collected 1,443 aluminum cans in 3 days. At this rate, how many cans will the class collect in 2 weeks, including Saturdays and Sundays?

c. A robot can weld 125 connections in $\frac{1}{2}$ hour. How long would it take this robot to weld 375 connections?

d. John wants to estimate the number of red and white chips in a box. He knows the box contains 100 red chips. Using the four samples below, estimate how many chips are in the box.

Sample 1	**Sample 2**
Number of red chips: 9	Number of red chips: 23
Number of red and white chips in sample: 25	Number of red and white chips in sample: 50
Sample 3	**Sample 4**
Number of red chips: 11	Number of red chips: 19
Number of red and white chips in sample: 30	Number of red and white chips in sample: 45

How Many Fish? Hands-On Activity

Materials

- Clear container
- 1,000 dry kidney beans (red beans)
- Unknown amount of dry navy beans (white beans)

Procedure

1. Ask students, "How do scientists count fish in a body of water? Can we ever know the exact number of fish in a body of water?"

2. Share the following explanation about the capture-recapture method. *Scientists use the capture-recapture method to estimate large populations, such as the number of fish in a body of water. This method is based on the theory that a total population can be estimated if a portion of the large population is measured. A population is measured by repeatedly capturing members, counting, tagging, and releasing them. The total population is then based on the proportion of the number tagged to the total sample.*

3. Using a clear container to represent a body of water, fill it with 1,000 dry kidney (red) beans or "tagged fish" and an unknown amount of dry navy (white) beans or "untagged fish," and mix the beans together.

4. Without telling the students the number of red beans, have students estimate the total number of beans in the container.

5. Create a stem-and-leaf plot of students' estimates on the graphing calculator.

6. Share the number of red beans in the container. Ask students, "Based on the number of red beans, how could we estimate the total number of beans?"

7. Ask students, "What do we know about the number of red beans?" *Answer: 1,000 red beans* "What do we know about the total number of beans?" *Answer: (unknown)* "How would a ratio be written that represents the number of red beans out of the total number of beans." *Answer:* 1000/x

8. Give each student a sample of red and white beans from the container. Have them represent their samples with a ratio for the number of red beans to the total number of beans. Have students set the ratios from steps 7 and 8 equal to each other and solve for the unknown.

9. Have students share their ratios. Create stem-and-leaf and box-and-whisker plots of students' data on the graphing calculator.

10. Ask students, "What is a good estimate of the number of beans in the container? What do the outliers tell us about the fish population?"

The Four Operations with Integers

Building Number Sense

Lesson Description

- Students will solve addition, subtraction, multiplication, and division problems that include positive and negative integers and a combination of these operations. This also includes those problems arising in concrete situations.

- Students will use manipulatives to understand how to compute addition, subtraction, multiplication, and division problems and use this knowledge to solve problems.

Materials

- Bi-color chips (yellow and red)
- *Practice! Practice! Integers* (page 60; nmbrs60.pdf)
- *More Integers* (pages 61–62; nmbrs61.pdf)
- Red and yellow large paper circles
- *Cover Up Numbers Game* (page 63; nmbrs63.pdf)
- TI-83/84 Plus Family Graphing Calculator or TI-73 Explorer™

Explaining the Concept/Using the Calculator

Step 1   Ask the students the following questions:

- What is a negative integer? *Answer: A number less than zero*
- Where are they on the number line? *Answer: To the left of zero*
- What is a positive integer? *Answer: A number greater than zero*
- Where are they on the number line? *Answer: To the right of zero*

Step 2   Use the counters to model how to add integers concretely.

- Explain that the yellow side of the counter represents positive integers and the red side represents negative integers.

- Explain that a zero pair is a yellow counter and red counter. Ask students why a yellow and a red counter together equal zero.

The Four Operations with Integers (cont.)

Building Number Sense

Explaining the Concept/Using the Calculator (cont.)

Step 3

Work the following problems with the students:

a. −2 + 1 = −1

- Have students set out two red counters and one yellow counter.

- Pull aside the zero pair. Explain that the remaining negative counter left is the answer.

Step 4

Have students use the graphing calculator to check their answers. Explain the difference between the negative sign and the subtraction keys.

- Press ⎣(-)⎦ to input the negative sign. Press ⎣2⎦.
- Press ➕ to input the operation. Press ⎣1⎦. Press **ENTER** to execute the command.

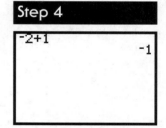

Step 5

b. −3 + 4 = 1

- Have students set out three red counters and four yellow counters.

- Pull aside the zero pairs. The positive counter left is the answer.

The Four Operations with Integers *(cont.)*

Building Number Sense

Explaining the Concept/Using the Calculator *(cont.)*

Step 6   Have students use the graphing calculator to check their answers.

- You may want to show students what happens when they use the subtraction key instead of the negative key. If students get a message, **ERR: SYNTAX**, select **2: Goto** and replace the subtraction sign with the negative sign.

- Press ⬚(-) to input the negative sign. Press ⬚3.

- Press ⬚+ to input the operation. Press ⬚4. Press **ENTER** to execute the command.

- Using the counters, have students work on problems **a–d** on *Practice! Practice! Integers* (page 60). Review the problems with the students.

Step 7   Use the counters to model how to subtract integers. Explain that the definition of subtraction is to add the opposite.

- Model the following problem with the students:

    c. $4 - 1 = 3$

- Have students set out four yellow counters to represent 4 then one yellow counter to represent 1.

- Explain to students that to add the opposite they need to switch the one yellow counter to a red counter.

- Pull aside the zero pair. Three positive counters remain.

The Four Operations with Integers *(cont.)*

Building Number Sense

Explaining the Concept/Using the Calculator *(cont.)*

Step 8 Have students use the graphing calculator to check the answer to the problem

> **c.** 4 − 1 = 3

Step 8
4−1   3

Step 9 Continue to model with the counters how to subtract integers. Remind students that the definition of subtraction is to add the opposite.

> **d.** 2 − 5 = −3

- Have students set out two yellow counters and five yellow counters.

- Add the opposite by switching the five yellow counters to five red counters.

- Pull aside the zero pairs. The three red counters that remain are the answer.

Step 10 Have students use the graphing calculator to check the answer to the problem.

> **d.** 2 − 5 = −3

Step 10
2−5   −3

Step 11 Using the counters, have students work problems **e–h** on *Practice! Practice! Integers* (page 60). Review the problems with the students.

- Have students check their answers, using the graphing calculator.

The Four Operations with Integers *(cont.)*

Building Number Sense

Explaining the Concept/Using the Calculator *(cont.)*

Step 12 Discuss the rules of multiplication and division for integers.

- When the signs are the same, the answer is positive.
- When the signs are different, the answer is negative.

Step 13 Have students share with a partner the different ways multiplication and division problems can be written. Then discuss the ways below, as a class.

Multiplication	Division
parentheses, e.g. ( ) dot, e.g. •	division symbol, e.g. ÷ fraction solidos, e.g. $-^{15}/_3$

Step 14 Have students work problems **i–p** on *Practice! Practice! Integers* (page 60). Review the problems with the students.

- Have students check their answers using the graphing calculator.

Step 15 Use problem **q–s** on *Practice! Practice! Integers* to discover if an answer will be positive or negative when multiplying even and odd number factors.

- The rule is that when multiplying an odd number of negative numbers, the answer is negative and when multiplying an even number of negative numbers, the answer is positive.

Applying the Concept

Step 1 Have students act out problem **e** on the activity sheet, *More Integers* (pages 61-62).

- Give student volunteers yellow paper circles to represent the yellow chips (positive integers) and red paper circles to represent the red chips (negative integers).
- Seven students will represent the seven yards gained with yellow chips.
- Four students will represent the four yards lost with red chips.
- Two students will represent the two yards lost with red chips.
- Eight students will represent the eight yards gained with yellow chips.

The Four Operations with Integers *(cont.)*

Building Number Sense

Applying the Concept *(cont.)*

Step 2

Follow the bulleted steps below to solve the problem.

- Have the students representing the seven yards gained and four yards lost come to the front of the class.
- Have the seven positive students stand in a line. Then have the four negative students stand in a line in front of the positive students.
- Have zero pair students sit down. Three positive students should remain in the front of the class.
- Repeat the process for the two yards lost and eight yards gained. At the end, there should be nine positive students in the front of the classroom.

Step 3

Have students use the graphing calculator to check the problem.

Step 4

Have students complete the activity sheet, *More Integers* (pages 61–62). Review the problems with the students.

Step 5

Have students play, *Cover Up Numbers Game* (page 63).

Extension Ideas

- To enhance mental math skills, have students solve the problems below.

  a. $-5 + 8 = 3$ **c.** $4 - 7 = -3$

  b. $(-5)(-3) = 15$ **d.** $\dfrac{20}{-4} = -5$

- Have students choose a company listed on the New York Stock Exchange (NYSE) and determine the week's net change for the company.

Name _____

Date _____

Practice! Practice! Integers

Directions: Use chips to solve the problems, then use the graphing calculator to check the answers.

a. $-1 + 6 =$ _____

b. $-3 + 7 =$ _____

c. $3 - 5 =$ _____

d. $4 - 9 =$ _____

e. $-5 + 2 =$ _____

f. $-8 + 4 =$ _____

g. $-3 - 3 =$ _____

h. $-3 - 9 =$ _____

Directions: Solve the problems using the rules for multiplying and dividing integers. Check the answers using the graphing calculator.

i. $-3(-6) =$ _____

j. $-8 \cdot 9 =$ _____

k. $\dfrac{-54}{-9} =$ _____

l. $-9 \div 3 =$ _____

m. $5 \cdot (-4) =$ _____

n. $-2(-12) =$ _____

o. $\dfrac{18}{-6} =$ _____

p. $30 \div (-5) =$ _____

q. For each problem in the table below, count the number of negative factors and record whether the answer will be positive or negative. Multiply the numbers and write the answers in the table.

Answer Positive or Negative	Problem	Answer
	$-5(-4)(-3) =$	
	$-2(-4)(-6)(-6) =$	
	$-9(-2)(-7) =$	
	$-3(-5)(-9)(-7) =$	

r. Is the answer positive or negative for an odd number of negative numbers?

_____

s. Is the answer positive or negative for an even number of positive numbers?

_____

#50026—Graphing Calculator Strategies, Middle School Math   © *Shell Education*

Name _____

Date _____

More Integers

Directions: Fill in each empty square with the sum of the pair of numbers beneath the square.

a.

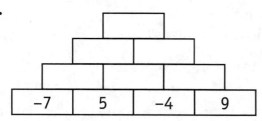

b.

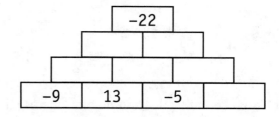

Directions: Fill in each empty square with the product of the pair of numbers beneath the square.

c.

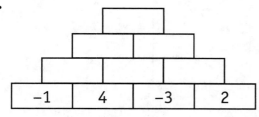

d.

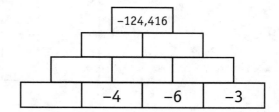

Directions: Write an expression for each of the following sentences, and then find the answer.

e. In a series of downs, a football team gained 7 yards, lost 4 yards, lost 2 yards, and gained 8 yards. What was the total gain or loss?

f. In a week, a given stock gained 5 points, dropped 12 points, dropped 3 points, gained 18 points, and dropped 10 points. What was the net change in the stock's worth?

Name _____

Date _____

More Integers (cont.)

Directions: Identify whether the following numbers are positive or negative, then solve.

g. $(-3)^5 =$ _____   Positive or negative? _____

h. $(-3)^8 =$ _____   Positive or negative? _____

Directions: In multiplication magic squares, the product of the integers in each row, each column, and each diagonal is the same number. Complete the multiplication magic squares below.

i.

		−64
	32	128
		−4

j.

−2		
3	−4	−18

Directions: Now create your own multiplication magic square.

k.

Cover Up Numbers Game

Directions: Play this game with 2 or 3 players. You will need 4 number cubes and a set of 32 markers for each player. Take turns following the steps below.

Rules

1. Roll 4 number cubes.

2. Use the numbers you rolled along with the operations of addition, subtraction, multiplication, and division to create a problem that equals a number on the game board.

3. Cover the number you created with a marker.

4. You get 1 point for every number you cover. If the number you cover is touching any other covered number, you get 2 points for each of those numbers.

5. If you cannot create an uncovered number on the game board, your turn is over.

6. Continue playing until all the numbers are covered.

7. The player with the highest number of points wins.

Game Board

−15	−14	−13	−12	−11	−10	−9	−8
−7	−6	−5	−4	−3	−2	−1	0
1	2	3	4	5	6	7	8
9	10	11	12	13	14	15	16

Using Patterns to Discover an Equation of a Line

Thinking Algebraically

Lesson Description

- Students will solve problems with linear functions that have integer values, write the equation, and graph the resulting ordered pairs of integers on a grid.
- Students will discover the equation of a line through patterns.

Materials

- *Patterns and Equations* (page 71; algbr71.pdf)
- *Practice! Practice! Equation of a Line* (page 72; algbr72.pdf)
- *Walking the Line* (page 73; algbr73.pdf)
- **Appendix C:** *Grid Paper* (1 cm) (page 202; appnd202.pdf)
- TI-83/84 Plus Family Graphing Calculator or TI-73 Explorer™

Explaining the Concept/Using the Calculator

Step 1

Use problems **a–f** on the activity sheet, *Patterns and Equations* (page 71), to model how to determine a rule for a pattern and how to write a linear expression to represent that rule.

- Ask students how many squares are being added in each row. *Answer: Add two*
- Ask students how many squares are in the sixth term? *Answer: 13*
- Have students determine the *nth* term, *2x + 1*. To help students write a linear equation, tell students that *x* represents the steps and *y* represents the number of squares.

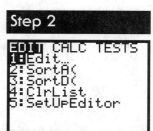

Step 2

Have the students input the data in the first table on *Patterns and Equations* into the List function on the graphing calculator.

- Press **STAT**. Press **1**. Input the row number in **L1** and the number of squares in **L2**.

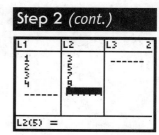

Using Patterns to Discover an Equation of a Line *(cont.)*

Thinking Algebraically

Explaining the Concept/Using the Calculator *(cont.)*

Step 3   Have students create a scatter plot in Plot 1.

- Press **2ND** and then **Y=** to access the Stat Plot editor. Press **1** to select **Plot1**.

- Select the following by highlighting them and pressing **ENTER**. Turn **On** the plot. By **Type**, select the scatter plot, which is the first icon. By **Xlist**, input **L1** (**2ND**, **1**). By **Ylist**, input **L2** (**2ND**, **2**). By **Mark**, select the first icon (square dot).

Step 4   Have students graph and analyze the scatter plot.

- Press **ZOOM** and then **6** to create a **ZStandard** window and to view the scatter plot.

- Ask students what was created on the graph. *Answer: A line*

Step 5   Have students determine the line of best fit.

- Press **STAT**. Move the cursor to the right once to highlight **CALC**.

- Press **4** to select **LinReg (ax+b)**. Press **ENTER**.

Step 6   Together, determine if the line of best fit is the same as the equation for the step and number of squares. The equation for the steps and number of squares is $y = 2x + 1$.

- Using two points, have students determine how many units up and across to get from one point to the other. *Answer: 2 units up and 1 unit to the right, positive moves along both the x- and y- axes equals a positive slope.*

- Have students write 2 units up and 1 across as a fraction, rise over run.

- Have students identify the rise-over-run fraction in the equation, $2x + 1$. Explain that this is the slope of a line.

Step 3

Step 4

Step 4 *(cont.)*

Step 5

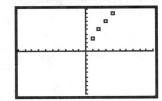

Step 5 *(cont.)*

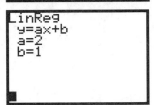

Using Patterns to Discover an Equation of a Line *(cont.)*

Thinking Algebraically

Explaining the Concept/Using the Calculator *(cont.)*

Step 7   Have students determine the y-intercept by graphing the equation, $2x + 1$.

- Press **Y=** to access the Y= screen.

- Input $2x + 1$. (Press the **X,T,ø,n** to access the variable x.)

- Press **GRAPH** to view a graph of the equation.

- Ask students at which point the line crosses the y-axis. *Answer: (0, 1).* Explain that this is the y–intercept.

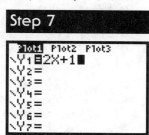

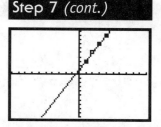

Step 8   Have students use the Table feature on the graphing calculator to check that the point is correct.

- Press **2ND** and then **GRAPH** to get the table of values for the equation, $y = 2x + 1$.

- Ask students to identify the y-intercept in the table. Students should explain how they identified it.

- Ask students, "What value in the equation represents the y-intercept?" *Answer: The 1 in the equation is the y-intercept.*

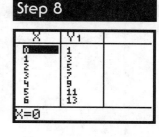

Step 9   Have students complete the second table and questions **g–l** on *Patterns and Equations* (page 71). Review the problems with the students.

Step 10   Have students complete the activity sheet, *Practice! Practice! Equation of a Line* (page 72). Review the problems with the students.

Using Patterns to Discover an Equation of a Line *(cont.)*

Thinking Algebraically

Applying the Concept

Step 1   Have students form small groups and give each group 2 pieces of grid paper (page 202). Students should divide the grid paper in half.

Step 2   Have each group draw an *x*- and *y*-axis on each grid.

Step 3   On one grid paper, have the group draw a line that passes through the point (0, 4). Have students write ordered pairs for two points on that line.

Step 4   Have a group share the line it created by giving you the two ordered pairs. Draw the line on the overhead or board. Ask students to identify the *y*-intercept and slope. Have another group share its line.

Step 5   On the other grid paper, have the group draw a line that passes through the point (0, −5). Have students write ordered pairs for two points on the line. Repeat **Steps 4–5** with the students.

Step 6   Have students complete *Walking the Line* (page 73). Review the problems with the students.

Extension Ideas
- Give students the equation, $y = 3x + 2$, and have them identify the slope and *y*-intercept.
- Have students find basic patterns in the surrounding environment, the classroom, nature, etc. Have students create a table for the pattern and graph a line to represent the pattern.

Patterns and Equations

Directions: Use the picture to complete the table; then answer the questions.

Row (x)	Number of Squares (y)
nth	

row 1

row 2

row 3

row 4

a. How many squares are added to each row in the pattern? _____

b. How many squares would be in the 6th row? _____

c. Write an equation to represent the *nth* row and record it in the table.

d. Create a scatter plot of the data on the graphing calculator. What is the linear regression?

_____

e. How many vertical and horizontal units are there between points? _____

f. What are the slope and *y*-intercept of the line? _____

Row (x)	Number of Squares (y)
nth	

row 1

row 2

row 3

row 4

g. How many squares are added to each figure in the pattern? _____

h. How many squares would be in the 6th figure? _____

i. Write an equation to represent the *nth* figure and record it in the table.

j. Create a scatter plot of the data on the graphing calculator. What is the linear regression?

_____

k. How many vertical and horizontal units are there between points? _____

l. What are the slope and the *y*-intercept of the line? _____

Practice! Practice! Equation of a Line

Directions: Use the picture to complete the table; then answer the questions.

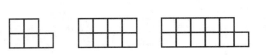

Figure (x)	Number of Squares (y)
nth	

a. How many squares are added to each figure in the pattern?

_____

b. How many squares in the 6th figure?

_____

c. Write an equation to represent the *nth* term and record it in the table.

_____

d. Create a scatter plot of the data on the graphing calculator. What is the linear regression?

_____

e. How many vertical and horizontal units are there between points?

_____

f. What is the slope of the line and the *y*-intercept?

_____

Directions: Use the graphing calculator to determine the equation for each table and then complete the table.

g.

x	y
1	1
2	3
3	5
0	
−1	

h.

x	y
1	2
2	5
3	8
0	
−1	

Name _____

Date _____

Walking the Line

Directions: Use the graph to determine the slope and *y*-intercept, then write the equation of the line.

I.

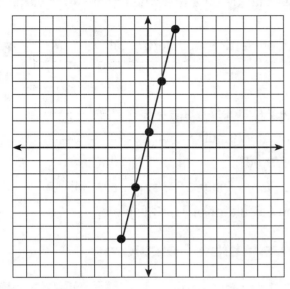

   a. slope: _____

   b. *y*-intercept: _____

   c. equation: _____

III.

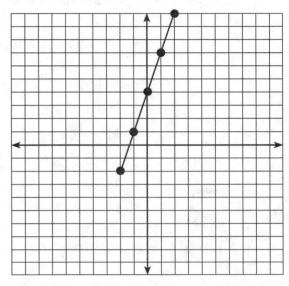

   g. slope: _____

   h. *y*-intercept: _____

   i. equation: _____

II.

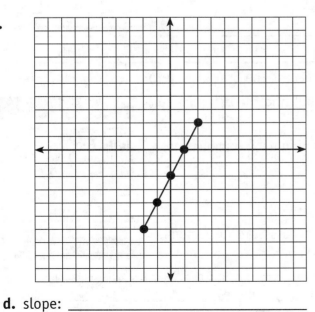

   d. slope: _____

   e. *y*-intercept: _____

   f. equation: _____

IV.

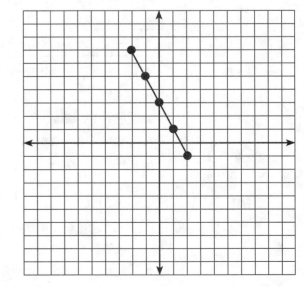

   j. slope: _____

   k. *y*-intercept: _____

   l. equation: _____

Representing Vertical & Horizontal Lines

Thinking Algebraically

Lesson Description

- Students will determine points that lie on a line when given an equation of a line.
- The students will write and graph vertical and horizontal lines.

Materials

- *Practice! Practice! Lines* (page 77; algbr77.pdf)
- *Where Do We Meet?* (page 78; algbr78.pdf)
- *Which Graph?* (page 79; algbr79.pdf)
- **Appendix C:** *Small Coordinate Planes* (page 204; appnd204.pdf)
- TI-83/84 Plus Family Graphing Calculator or TI-73 Explorer™

Explaining the Concept/Using the Calculator

Step 1 Have students use their arms to practice representing vertical and horizontal lines.

Step 2 Have students input the ordered pairs into the Stat List editor. Use L1 for the *x*-coordinates and L2 for the *y*-coordinates.

| (5, −5) (5, −4) (5, −3) (5, −2) (5, −1) (5, 0) (5, 1) (5, 2) (5, 3) (5, 4) (5, 5) |

- Press **STAT** and then **ENTER** to access the Stat List editor.
- Clear data from lists by highlighting the list name and pressing **CLEAR** and then **ENTER**.
- Input the ordered pairs by typing each number and pressing **ENTER**.

Step 3 Have students create a line graph in Plot 1.

- Press **2ND** and then **Y=** to access Stat Plots menu. Press **1** to select the **Plot1**.
- Select the following settings by highlighting the setting and pressing **ENTER** Select **On**. By **Type**, select the first icon. By **Xlist**, input **L1** (**2ND**, **1**) and by **Ylist**, input **L2** (**2ND**, **2**). By **Mark**, select the square (the first icon).

Representing Vertical & Horizontal Lines *(cont.)*

Thinking Algebraically

Explaining the Concept/Using the Calculator *(cont.)*

Step 4
Press **ZOOM** and then the **6** to create a **ZStandard** window and display the graph. Then, ask students the following questions about the graph.

- Is it a vertical or horizontal line? *Answer: Vertical*
- What do you notice about the ordered pairs for the vertical line? *Answer: All of the x-coordinates are 5*
- What is the equation for this line? *Answer: x = 5*

Step 5
Have students input the following ordered pairs into **L3** and **L4** of the Stat List editor.

> (–5, –3) (–4, –3) (–3, –3) (–2, –3) (–1, –3) (0, –3)
> (1, –3) (2, –3) (3, –3) (4, –3) (5, –3)

- Press **STAT** and then **ENTER** to access the **List**.
- Enter the ordered pairs by typing each number and pressing **ENTER**.

Step 6
Have students create a line graph in Plot 2.

- Press **2ND** and then **Y=** to access the Stat Plot menu. Press **2** to select **Plot2**.
- Select the following settings by highlighting the setting and pressing **ENTER**. Select **On**. By **Type**, select the first icon and press **ENTER**. By **Xlist**, input **L3** (**2ND**, **3**) and by **Ylist**, input **L2** (**2ND**, **4**). By **Mark**, select the square (the first icon).

Step 7
Press **GRAPH** to view the line.

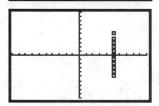

Step 4 (cont.)

Step 5

Step 6

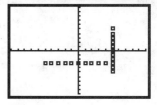

Step 7

Representing Vertical & Horizontal Lines *(cont.)*

Thinking Algebraically

Explaining the Concept/Using the Calculator *(cont.)*

Step 8   Ask students the following questions about the line in Plot 2:

- Did the new set of ordered pairs create a vertical or a horizontal line? *Answer: Horizontal*
- What do you notice about the ordered pairs for the horizontal line? *Answer: All the y-coordinates are –3.*
- What is the equation for this line? *Answer: y = –3*
- At which point do the two lines meet? *Answer: (5, –3)*

Step 9   Have students complete the activity sheet, *Practice! Practice! Lines* (page 77). Review the problems with the students.

Applying the Concept

Step 1   Place a transparency coordinate grid on top of a picture, wallpaper, or fabric.

Step 2   Divide students into small groups and give them a few minutes to list the locations of the vertical and horizontal lines in the picture, wallpaper, or fabric.

- Have students write down the coordinates of the points of intersection.

Step 3   Discuss those lines and points of intersection.

Step 4   Have students complete the activity sheet, *Where Do We Meet?* (page 78). Review the problems with the students.

Step 5   Have students complete the activity sheet, *Which Graph?* (page 79). Review the problems with the students.

Extension Ideas

- To enhance mental math skills, give students ordered pairs, such as (6, 7) (6, 9) (6, 3) (6, 1) and ask students if the plotted points would form a horizontal or a vertical line. *Answer: Vertical*
- Give another set of ordered pairs that would create a horizontal line. Ask students where the two lines will intersect.

Name _____

Date _____

Practice! Practice! Lines

Directions: Determine if the given points will create a vertical or a horizontal line. Then graph the line on the coordinate plane and the graphing calculator. Record the equation of the line.

I.

x	y
1	−4
1	−3
1	1
1	2

a. Type of line: _____

b. Equation of line: _____

II.

x	y
−7	−4
−4	−4
5	−4
9	−4

c. Type of line: _____

d. Equation of line: _____

III.

x	y
7	−6
7	−2
7	4
7	8

e. Type of line: _____

f. Equation of line: _____

IV.

x	y
−7	2
−5	2
1	2
8	2

g. Type of line: _____

h. Equation of line: _____

Lines I & II

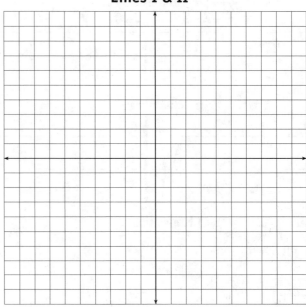

Lines III & IV

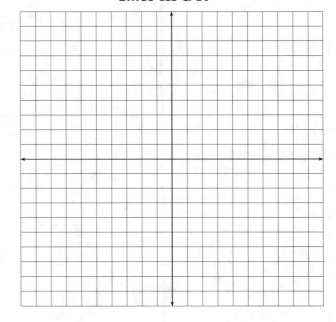

i. At which point does the line intersect with the line just drawn? _____

Name _____

Date _____

Where Do We Meet?

Directions: List four ordered pairs for the given equations. To find the point of intersection, graph the two lines on your graphing calculator and on the coordinate grids below.

a. $x = -3$ $y = -6$

x	y	x	y

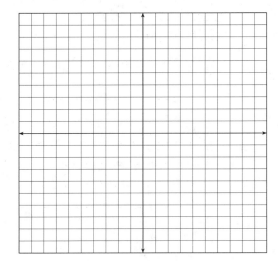

b. Where do the two lines intersect? _____

c. Graph the lines.

d. $x = 5$ $y = -2$

x	y	x	y

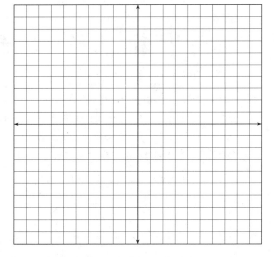

e. Where do the two lines intersect? _____

f. Graph the lines.

g. $x = -7$ $y = 4$

x	y	x	y

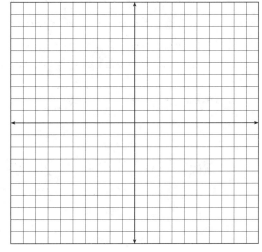

h. Where do the two lines intersect? _____

i. Graph the lines.

Name _____

Date _____

Which Graph?

Directions: Create a graph to represent the given situations and list the ordered pairs in the tables.

I. Mr. Jones is painting a stripe along his wall. He starts 3 feet off the floor and 3 feet from the door. Later, he is 3 feet off the floor and 5 feet from the door, then 3 feet off the floor and 7 feet from the door. He finishes 3 feet off the floor and 9 feet from the door.

a. List the four ordered pairs and graph the line.

x	y

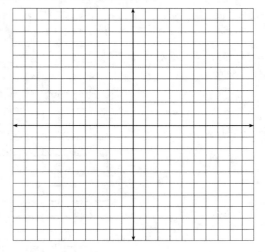

b. What type of line did Mr. Jones create? _____

c. Write an equation to represent the line. _____

II. Samantha was watching a spider crawl along the wall. The spider started 2 feet from the ceiling and 2 feet from the corner of the room. A few seconds later, it was 4 feet from the ceiling and 2 feet from the corner. Later, it was 6 feet from the ceiling and 2 feet from the corner, and it finally stopped 8 feet from the ceiling and 2 feet from the corner.

d. List the four ordered pairs and graph the line.

x	y

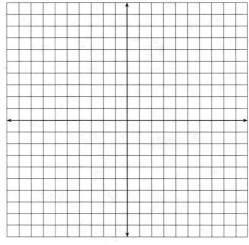

e. What type of line did the spider create? _____

f. Write an equation to represent the line. _____

Name _____

Date _____

Which Graph? *(cont.)*

III. Jose and Shawna are running from different locations. They will run the same distance at the same speed. Jose starts at Meyer Park and will run east. Shawna starts at Fairfield Park and will run north.

Meyer Park

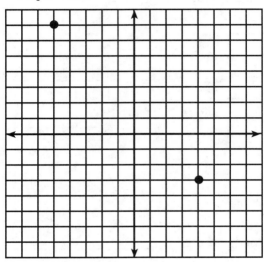

Fairfield Park

g. List four ordered pairs for Shawna's run.

x	y

h. List four ordered pairs for Jose's run.

x	y

i. Write an equation to represent Jose's run.

_____

j. Write the equation to represent Shawna's run.

_____

k. Graph the two points on your graphing calculator. At which point might Jose's and Shawna's paths cross?

_____

Writing and Evaluating Algebraic Expressions

Thinking Algebraically

Lesson Description

- Students will write algebraic expressions, using up to three variables to represent a given scenario, and will evaluate those expressions.
- Students will substitute values for variables and solve.

Materials

- *Practice! Practice! Expressions* (page 84; algbr84.pdf)
- *Applying Expressions* (page 85; algbr85.pdf)
- *Invest It!* (page 86; algbr86.pdf)
- TI-83/84 Plus Family Graphing Calculator or TI-73 Explorer™

Explaining the Concept

Step 1

Ask students the following questions:

- What is an expression? What is an example of an expression? *Answer: A mathematical statement with a combination of variables, numbers, and symbols.*
- What does it mean to evaluate an expression? *Answer: To find the value of the variables in an expression*

Step 2

Write the problem below on the overhead or board.

$$\blacktriangle + \blacksquare \times 2$$

- Have each student work with a partner to pick a value for each shape and evaluate the expressions.
- Have student volunteers model how to substitute the values for the triangle and square and evaluate the expressions.

Step 3

Write the following expressions on the overhead or board:

$$ab \qquad a + b \qquad a - b$$

- Ask students if the expressions can be solved and why or why not. *Answer: No, because the values for a and b are not given*

Writing and Evaluating Algebraic Expressions *(cont.)*

Thinking Algebraically

Explaining the Concept *(cont.)*

Step 4

Ask a student volunteer to give a value for *a* and *b*.

- Write these values on the board or overhead. Have students substitute values to evaluate the expressions in **Step 3**.

- Review the values for the expressions with the students.

Using the Calculator

Step 1

Explain that to use a graphing calculator to evaluate an expression such as *ab*, values first must be stored for the given variables. For *a*, store 13.56 and for *b*, store 26.08.

- Type **13.56** and then press [STO►]. Press [ALPHA] and then [MATH] to input the variable *a*.

- Press [ENTER] to execute the command.

- Repeat the steps to input **26.08**, except press [ALPHA] and then [APPS] to access the variable *B*.

- Press [ENTER] to execute the command.

```
Step 1
13.56→A
              13.56
26.08→B
              26.08
■
```

Step 2

Evaluate the expression *ab*.

- Input the variable *a* by pressing [ALPHA], [MATH]. Input the operation [×].

- Press [ALPHA], [APPS] to access the variable *b*. Press [ENTER] to execute the command.

- Have students evaluate the expressions *a + b* and *a − b*.

```
Step 2
A*B
            353.6448
A+B
              39.64
A−B
             -12.52
```

Step 3

Have students complete the activity sheet, *Practice! Practice! Expressions* (page 84). Review the problems with the students.

Writing and Evaluating Algebraic Expressions *(cont.)*

Thinking Algebraically

Applying the Concept

Step 1
Have students complete the activity sheet, *Applying Expressions* (page 85).

Step 2
Review the problems used in *Applying Expressions*, and ask students the following questions about the tables.

- What kind of information is given in the tables and how is it organized?
- Why are tables used to solve problems?
- How did the tables help you solve the problems?

Step 3
Have students complete *Invest It!* (page 86).

- Read the activity sheet together.
- Discuss the information needed to solve the problem.
- Using problem **II** on *Invest It!* (page 86) have students create two tables for Build-A-Pet Workshop and Wally World Company.
- Discuss the information to be included in the tables and how the tables can be organized.

Build-A-Pet Workshop

Day	Number of Shares (a)	Closing Price	Cost of Shares
Mon.		$30.15	
Tues.		$29.35	
Wed.		$31.45	
Thurs.		$28.95	
Fri.		$30.75	

Wally World Company

Day	Number of Shares (b)	Closing Price	Cost of Shares
Mon.		$26.75	
Tues.		$27.75	
Wed.		$26.35	
Thurs.		$26.15	
Fri.		$26.95	

Extension Ideas

- To enhance mental math skills, give students a value for a and b then have them evaluate the following expressions.

$$ab \qquad a + b \qquad a - b$$

- Have students create problems like those given in the **Explaining the Concept** section (pages 81–82). Use the problems in future math lessons.
- Have students use the Internet or newspaper to track the value of the shares for two companies' stocks and create a graph to represent the gains and losses.

Name _____

Date _____

Practice! Practice! Expressions

Directions: Input the values into the graphing calculator for each variable and solve the given expressions. Round answers to the nearest hundredth.

| $c = 15.5$ $d = 6.25$ $e = 13.75$ |

a. $\dfrac{(d + e)}{c}$ _____

b. cde _____

c. $(d - e)c$ _____

d. $\dfrac{(d + e)}{d} + \dfrac{de}{c}$ _____

Directions: Using the values for c, d, and e, create two expressions and then have a partner evaluate the expressions.

e. _____

f. _____

Directions: Input the values into the graphing calculator for each variable and solve the given expressions. Round answers to the nearest hundredth.

| $g = \dfrac{4}{5}$ $h = \dfrac{1}{4}$ $i = \dfrac{5}{8}$ |

g. $g + h + i$ _____

h. ghi _____

i. $gh + i$ _____

j. $\dfrac{gh}{g} + gi$ _____

Directions: Using the values for g, h, and i, create two expressions and then have a partner evaluate the expressions.

k. _____

l. _____

Directions: Read the information and then answer the questions.

Emma works for Designer Footwear and receives a 10% discount on any purchase.

m. How much will she pay for a pair of shoes that normally costs $37.00? Explain your steps.

_____

n. How can she calculate her discount for any shoe in one step? _____

_____

o. Think about this! What percent of the shoe price is she paying? What happens when you multiply that percent by the shoe price? _____

_____

Name _____

Date _____

Applying Expressions

Directions: Use the graphing calculator to solve the problems below.

a. Jane is installing a rectangular pool this summer. She wants its length to be 21³/₄ ft, and its width to be 15¹/₄ ft. The volume of the pool can range from 1600 ft³ to 2700 ft³. Calculate possible depths for her pool and record them in the table below. Use L for the value of the length and W for the value of the width on the graphing calculator. Round the volume to the nearest whole number.

Length	Width	Height	Volume
$21\frac{3}{4}$ ft	$15\frac{1}{4}$ ft		
$21\frac{3}{4}$ ft	$15\frac{1}{4}$ ft		
$21\frac{3}{4}$ ft	$15\frac{1}{4}$ ft		
$21\frac{3}{4}$ ft	$15\frac{1}{4}$ ft		

b. You are an employee at a coffee shop where you receive a 15% discount. You work 4 days a week. While on your breaks, you have a drink and dessert. You budget $16.50 a week to spend on these snacks. Plan a menu for your breaks. Assign a variable for each menu item and the discount. Then write an expression to represent the cost of a drink and dessert each working day. Use the graphing calculator to evaluate the expressions to get your daily total.

Variable	Menu Item	Price
	Hot Chocolate	$2.25
	Chai Tea	$3.25
	Apple Cinnamon Scone	$2.45
	Chocolate Chip Muffin	$1.75
	Discount	

Monday		Wednesday		Friday		Sunday	
Drink	**Dessert**	**Drink**	**Dessert**	**Drink**	**Dessert**	**Drink**	**Dessert**
Expression:		Expression:		Expression:		Expression:	
Total:		Total:		Total:		Total:	

Invest It!

Directions: Follow the steps below. Answer the questions on a separate piece of paper.

I. Your grandfather, who is a stockbroker, gave you $500 for your birthday on Sunday to invest in stocks. After researching companies listed on the New York Stock Exchange (NYSE), you invested in Build-A-Pet Workshop, Inc. (BAP) and Wally World Company (WLW). At the time, Build-A-Pet Workshop, Inc. was $29.60 per share, and Wally World Company was $26.55 per share.

   a. Decide how many shares of each company you want to purchase with $500. Multiply the number of shares times the selling price to equal the purchasing price.

   Number of BAP shares _____ x $29.60 = _____ (purchasing price)

   Number of WLW shares _____ x $26.55 = _____ (purchasing price)

   b. On the graphing calculator, store the number of shares purchased for Build-A-Pet for variable a. Store the number of shares purchased for Wally World for variable b.

II. Over the next week, you recorded the closing price for both companies. Determine how much your stocks were worth each day.

   c. The daily closing prices for Build-A-Pet Workshop are listed below. On a separate piece of paper, create a table to record the number of shares purchased (a) the cost of the share that day, and the total value of your shares. Start on Sunday when you bought the stocks.

Monday—$30.15	Tuesday—$29.35	Wednesday—$31.45
Thursday—$28.95	Friday—$30.75	

   d. On the graphing calculator, multiply the closing prices by the variable a to get the cost of shares for that day. Record the data in your table.

   e. Which days would give you the highest profit and greatest loss? By how much?

   f. The daily closing prices for Wally World are listed below. On a separate piece of paper, create a table to record the number of shares purchased (b) and the value of the shares.

Monday—$26.75	Tuesday—$27.75	Wednesday—$26.35
Thursday—$26.15	Friday—$26.95	

   g. Which days would give you the highest profit and greatest loss? By how much?

Identifying the Point of Intersection

Thinking Algebraically

Lesson Description

- Students will use algebra to solve a system of two linear equations with two variables and interpret the answer graphically.

- The students will graph two linear equations and determine the point of intersection.

Materials

- Transparency of a large coordinate plane (1 per group)
- Pictures, designs, or wallpaper with intersecting lines (1 per group)
- *Practice! Practice! Intersecting Lines* (page 91; algbr91.pdf)
- *Applying Intersecting Lines* (page 92; algbr92.pdf)
- **Appendix C:** *Small Coordinate Planes* (1 per group) (page 204; appnd204.pdf)
- TI-83/84 Plus Family Graphing Calculator or TI-73 Explorer™

Explaining the Concept

Step 1   Ask students the following question:

- What are intersecting lines? *Answer: Lines that have one or more points in common*

Step 2   Have students form small groups. Give each small group a picture, wallpaper, or fabric and place a transparency of a large coordinate plane on top of it.

Step 3   Give groups a few minutes to list the intersecting lines in the picture, wallpaper, or fabric.

- Have groups list points of intersections.

- Ask students how they would identify the point of intersection if these two lines were graphed on a coordinate plane. *Answer: It is the point at which both lines share the same coordinate pair.*

Step 4   Have each group present a graph of intersecting lines from their pictures to the rest of the class.

Identifying the Point of Intersection *(cont.)*

Thinking Algebraically

Using the Calculator

Step 1   Have students input the following ordered pairs into L1 and L2. Or use ordered pairs from a set of intersecting lines presented by one of the groups in the previous step.

> (1, 6) (2, 8) (3, 10) (4, 12)

- Input the *x*-values in **L1** and *y*-values in **L2**. Press **ENTER** after each.

Step 2   Have students input the following ordered pairs into L3 and L4.

> (1, 7) (2, 8) (3, 9) (4, 10)

- Input the *x*-values in **L3** and *y*-values in **L4**. Press **ENTER** after each.

Step 3   Have students create a line graph in Plot 1 using L1 for the XList and L2 for the YList.

- Press **2ND** and then **Y=** to access the Stat Plot menu. Press **1** to select **Plot1**.

- Select the following settings by highlighting the icon and pressing **ENTER**. Select **On**; by **Type**, select the 2nd icon (line graph); by **Mark**, select the first icon.

Step 4   Repeat Step 3 to create a line graph in **Plot2** using **L3** for the **Xlist** and **L4** for the **Ylist**.

Step 5   Have students graph the two lines.

- Press **ZOOM** and then **9** to create a **ZoomStat** window and to view the graph.

- Press **TRACE** and use the left and right arrow keys to view points along the line.

- Determine the point at which the two lines intersect. *Answer: (2, 8)*

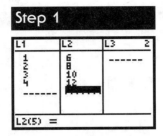

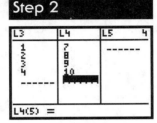

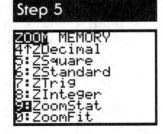

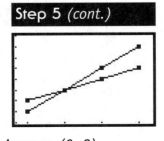

#50026—*Graphing Calculator Strategies, Middle School Math*   © *Shell Education*

Identifying the Point of Intersection (cont.)

Thinking Algebraically

Applying the Concept

Step 1 Write the following problem on the board or overhead: *Sue is trying to determine which rental plan is better. Rental A has a one–time fee of $10 and $1.50 per rental. Rental B has a one-time fee of $12 and $1.25 per rental.*

- Have students write an equation for each rental plan. *Answer: Rental A : y = 1.50x + 10 and Rental B : y = 1.25x + 12*

Step 2 Have students input the equations into the Y= screen.

- Press [Y=].

- Turn off the stat plots by highlighting the plot and pressing [ENTER] to unselect them.

- By y_1, input 1.50*x* + 10 and by **Y₂**, input 1.25*x* + 12. Press [X,T,Ø,n] to insert *x*.

Step 3 Before graphing the equations, have students change the values of the window range.

- Press [WINDOW]. Input the values shown in the screen shot to the right.

- Press [GRAPH] to view the intersection.

- Ask students at which point the lines intersect. Students may have a hard time determining the point from the graph.

Step 4 Model how to use the Table feature to find the point of intersection.

- Have students press [2ND] and then [GRAPH].

- Ask students how they can use the table to determine the point of intersection. *Answer: Scroll until they find the same value of Y₁ and Y₂. The point of intersection is (8, 22).*

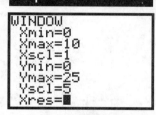

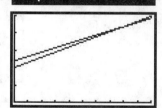

Identifying the Point of Intersection *(cont.)*

Thinking Algebraically

Applying the Concept *(cont.)*

Step 5 Ask students the following questions:

- What do the values for *x* represent? *Answer: The number of rentals*
- What do the values for *y* represent? *Answer: The total amount for the fee and the number of rentals*
- What does the point of intersection represent? *Answer: When both rental plans cost the same amount*
- Which one is the better deal? Have students explain their answers. *Answer: If one rents less than 8 rentals, Rental A is the better deal. If one rents more than 8 rentals, Rental B is the better deal.*

Step 6 Have students complete the activity sheet, *Practice! Practice! Intersecting Lines* (page 91). Review the problems with the students.

Step 7 Have students complete the activity sheet, *Applying Intersecting Lines*, (page 92). Review the problems with the students.

Extension Ideas

- Have students look in the newspaper and magazines to find graphs with intersecting lines. Have students explain what each graph represents.

Name _____

Date _____

Practice! Practice! Intersecting Lines

Directions: Identify the points of intersection in the graphs below.

a.

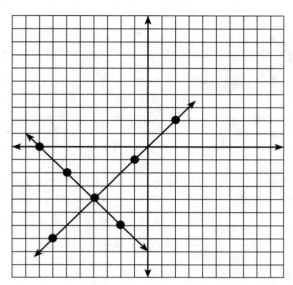

Point of Intersection: _____

b.

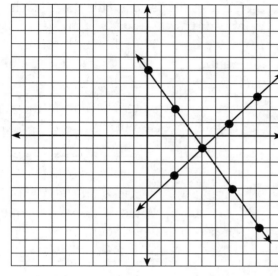

Point of Intersection: _____

Directions: Use the given equations to complete the tables below. Graph the lines on the graphing calculator to determine the point of intersection.

$y = 5x + 3$

x	y
−1	
0	
1	
2	

$y = 3x + 7$

x	y
−1	
0	
1	
2	

c. What is the point of intersection? _____

Directions: Solve the application problem below.

Rose runs 4 miles per hour and Rick runs 5 miles per hour. Rose starts running at mile marker 8. Rick starts running at mile marker 5. Answer the questions to determine at which mile marker Rose and Rick will meet.

d. Write equations to represent Rose's and Rick's runs.

_____

e. What do the x and y values represent?

_____

f. Graph both equations on the graphing calculator. At which mile marker will Rose and Rick meet?

_____

Name _____

Date _____

Applying Intersecting Lines

Directions: Solve the problems below. Graph the lines on the graphing calculator and below.

I. Greg gets $.35 per day plus $8.25 each month for his allowance. Frank gets $.25 per day plus $9.55 each month for his allowance.

    a. Write equations to represent Greg's and Frank's allowances. What do the x and y-values represent?

_____

    b. Graph the equations on the graphing calculator. When will Greg and Frank make the same amount?

_____

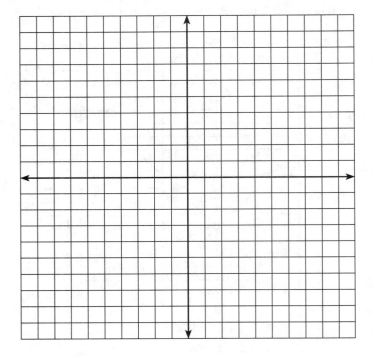

II. Tammy needs to rent a car. Rental A costs $55.50 plus $.55 per mile to rent. Rental B costs $66.50 plus $.35 per mile to rent.

    c. Write equations to represent the cost for Rental A and Rental B. What do the x- and y-values represent?

_____

    d. Graph the two equations. After how many miles will both rental companies cost the same?

_____

    e. Which rental company is cheaper if Tammy travels 49 miles? 68 miles?

_____

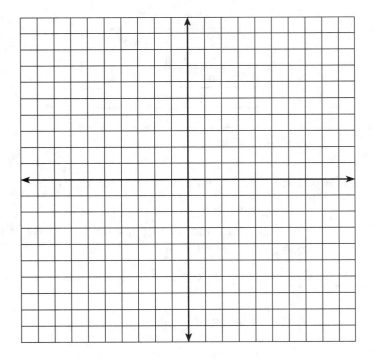

Analyzing Data

Creating Stem-and-Leaf Plots

Analyzing Data

Lesson Description

- Students will utilize various forms to display a single set of data or compare two sets of data, including a stem-and-leaf plot.
- Students will create a stem-and-leaf plot when given a set of data.

Materials

- *Practice! Practice! Stem-and-Leaf Plot* (page 99; data99.pdf)
- *Ballpark Capacity* (page 100; data100.pdf)
- 5 cereal boxes
- *What Is in Your Cereal Box?* (page 101-102; data101.pdf)
- TI-83/84 Plus Family Graphing Calculator or TI-73 Explorer™

Explaining the Concept

Step 1

Ask students the following questions:

- What are stem-and-leaf plots? *Answer: They organize data from least to greatest, using the digits of the greatest place value to group data.*
- How are mean, median, and mode calculated? *Answer: Mean: add the data and divide by the number of numbers. Median: write the data from least to greatest and find the middle number. Mode: identify the most repeated number in a data set.*

Step 2

Read the following scenario and write the data on the board.
DeAnna asked the residents in her apartment building their ages. She gathered the following data and decided the best way to display the greatest, least, and median ages would be to create a stem-and-leaf plot.

[58, 39, 22, 54, 47, 64, 44, 21, 50, 51, 36, 35]

Step 3

Follow the steps below to model how to create a stem-and-leaf plot.

Resident Ages

Tens (Stem)	Ones (Leaf)
2	1, 2
3	5, 6, 9
4	4, 7
5	0, 1, 4, 8
6	4

1. Draw the plot. Write the data in order from least to greatest.

2. On the left side, write the tens digits from least to greatest. These are the *stems*.

3. On the right side, write all the ones digits that go with each stem in order from least to greatest. These are the *leaves*.

Creating Stem-and-Leaf Plots *(cont.)*

Analyzing Data

Using the Calculator

Step 1   Read to students the following scenario and write the data on the board.

Justin is recording daily summer temperatures in various geographic regions for a scientific study on global warming. For each day that he collects data, he creates a stem-and-leaf plot of the temperatures to more easily view the greatest, least, and median values in his data set. Create a stem-and-leaf plot using the temperature data that Justin collected on June 24th.

$$\begin{bmatrix} 97,\ 99,\ 81,\ 78,\ 73,\ 95,\ 63,\ 97,\ 64,\ 94, \\ 85,\ 83,\ 86,\ 87,\ 78,\ 81,\ 93,\ 86,\ 83,\ 71 \end{bmatrix}$$

- Have students create a stem-and-leaf plot on a piece of paper.

Tens	Ones
6	3, 4
7	1, 3, 8, 8
8	1, 1, 3, 3, 5, 6, 6, 7
9	3, 4, 5, 7, 7, 9

Step 2   Draw the stem-and-leaf plot on the board or overhead and analyze the plot with the students by asking the following questions.

- What are the lowest and highest temperatures?
  Answer: 63 and 99

- What is the median? *Answer: 84*

- Does this data set have a mode? *Answer: 78, 81, 83, 86, and 97*

Step 3

```
EDIT CALC TESTS
1:Edit…
2:SortA(
3:SortD(
4:ClrList
5:SetUpEditor
```

Step 3 *(cont.)*

L1	L2	L3	1
97	------	------	
99			
81			
78			
73			
95			
63			

L1(1)=97

Step 3   On the graphing calculator, have students enter the data given in **Step 1** into the Stat List editor.

- Press [STAT] and then [ENTER] to access the Stat List editor.

- To delete data from a list, highlight the name of the list and press [CLEAR] and then [ENTER].

- Input the data into **L1** by typing each number and pressing [ENTER].

Creating Stem-and-Leaf Plots *(cont.)*

Analyzing Data

Using the Calculator *(cont.)*

Step 4

Have students calculate the mean and median on the graphing calculator.

- Press **2ND** and then **MODE** to return to the Home screen.

- Access the List by pressing **2ND** and then **STAT** and move the cursor to highlight **MATH**.

- Press **3** to select **mean(**.

- Input **L1** by pressing **2ND** then **1**. Press **)** to close the expression. Press **ENTER** to execute the command.

Step 5

Have students calculate the median by following the same steps listed above.

- Except after highlighting **MATH**, press **4** to select **median(**.

- Input **L1**, press **)** to close the expression, and press **ENTER** to execute the command.

Step 6

Have students calculate the range of the data set.

- On the Home screen of the graphing calculator, subtract the smaller number from the larger number to find the range.

- Input **99–63**. Press **9** **9** **−** **6** **3** .

- Press **ENTER** to evaluate the expression, which should equal **36**.

Step 7

Have students calculate the mode of the data set.

- On scratch paper, write the data in numerical order.

- Circle the numbers that repeat most frequently. *Answer: 78, 81, 83, 86, 97*

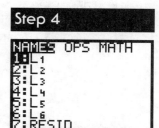

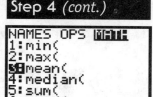

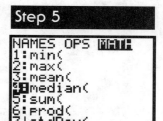

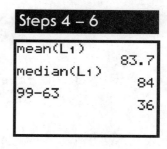

Creating Stem-and-Leaf Plots *(cont.)*

Analyzing Data

Using the Calculator *(cont.)*

Step 8   Have students complete the activity sheet, *Practice! Practice! Stem-and-Leaf Plot* (page 99) in small groups.

- Assign each group a different problem and have them record their stem-and-leaf plots and answers to the questions on chart paper. Students should also write down any short-cuts or steps they used on the graphing calculator.
- Have students walk around the room to compare their answers to those of the other groups.

Step 9   Have students complete the *Ballpark Capacity* (page 100). Review the problems with the students.

Applying the Concept

Step 1   Before beginning the activity, *What Is in Your Cereal Box?* (pages 101–102), place the cereal boxes used for the activity in front of the class.

Step 2   In small groups, have students discuss which cereal they believe contains more fat, cholesterol, dietary fiber, and sugar.

- Have students share their predictions with the class and record students' predictions on the board or overhead.

Step 3   Have students complete the *What Is in Your Cereal Box?* (pages 101–102). Review the problems with the students.

Step 4   After completing the activity, have the students discuss, in their groups, the information gathered and if their predictions were correct.

Extension Ideas

- Have students research sports statistics that can be displayed using a stem-and-leaf plot.
- Bring two weeks' worth of coupons from the Sunday paper. Have students create stem-and-leaf plots for each set of coupons. Have students decide if each week provides the same amount of savings.

Practice! Practice! Stem-and-Leaf Plot

Directions: On a separate piece of paper, create stem-and-leaf plots to represent the data given in the scenarios below. Then analyze the stem-and-leaf plots by answering the questions.

I. This summer you decided to get odd jobs to save for a new bike, which costs $350. You decided to keep a log of your daily earnings. In one month, you earned the following amounts.

> $11, $9, $15, $18, $20, $11, $9, $6, $12, $16,
>
> $11, $18, $19, $14, $15, $20, $25, $13, $12, $15

  a. Draw the stem-and-leaf plot on a separate piece of paper.

  b. What are the mean, median, mode, and range of the data set?

  _____

  c. How much more do you need to earn to purchase the new bike? Estimate how many more days you have to work to purchase the bike.

  _____

II. Your mother cut a stack of coupons from the Sunday paper. Your mother asked you to create a stem-and-leaf plot to display the value of the coupons, so she could determine the mean, median, mode, and range of savings. The following data set shows the value of the coupons.

> $1.50, $0.75, $0.35, $1.00, $0.45, $0.30, $0.75,
>
> $0.25, $0.25, $1.50, $0.75, $0.45, $0.30, $0.50

  d. Draw the stem-and-leaf plot on a separate piece of paper.

  e. What are the mean, median, mode, and range of the data set?

  _____

  f. Each Monday your mother grocery shops and uses all the coupons from the paper. Based on the data collected, estimate how much money she will save in a month. Justify your answer.

  _____

III. Mrs. Miller's class recorded the outside temperature at 1 p.m. every day for 2 weeks. The following temperatures were recorded.

> 79, 83, 85, 86, 85, 86, 87, 78, 88, 83

  g. Draw the stem-and-leaf plot on a separate piece of paper.

  h. What are the mean, median, mode, and range of the data set?

Name _____

Date _____

Ballpark Capacity

Directions: Below is a list of National League Ballparks and their seating capacities. Use the information to create a stem-and-leaf plot and find the mean, median, mode, and range.

Ballpark	Team	Seats	Ballpark	Team	Seats
AT&T Park	San Francisco	40,800	Miller Park	Milwaukee	43,000
Busch Stadium	St. Louis	50,345	Minute Maid Park	Houston	42,000
Chase Field	Arizona	48,500	PETCO Park	San Diego	42,445
Citizens Bank Park	Philadelphia	43,500	PNC Park	Pittsburg	38,127
Coors Field	Colorado	50,381	RFK Stadium	Washington	56,500
Dolphins Stadium	Florida	42,531	Shea Stadium	New York	55,777
Great American Ballpark	Cincinnati	42,059	Turner Field	Atlanta	50,062
Dodger Stadium	Los Angeles	56,000	Wrigley Field	Chicago	38,902

a. Draw the stem-and-leaf plot below.

b. Use the data above to find the mean, median, mode, and range.

mean: _____   median: _____

mode: _____   range: _____

c. Research the seating capacity for the American League Ballparks. On a separate piece of paper, make a table to organize your data and create a stem-and-leaf plot to find the mean, median, mode, and range of the data.

Name _____

Date _____

What Is in Your Cereal Box?

Directions: Using at least 5 cereal boxes, use the nutrition facts label to create a stem-and-leaf plot for the total fat, cholesterol, dietary fiber, and sugars in one serving. Use the information gathered to find the mean, median, mode, and range.

a. For each kind of cereal, record the amount of total fat in one serving.

Name of Cereal	Total Fat

b. Create a stem-and-leaf plot for the total fat in each cereal.

c. Find the mean, median, mode, and range for the total fat.

mean: _____   median: _____

mode: _____   range: _____

d. For each kind of cereal, record the amount of cholesterol in one serving.

Name of Cereal	Cholesterol

e. Create a stem-and-leaf plot to represent the amount of cholesterol in each cereal.

f. Find the mean, median, mode, and range for the cholesterol in all five cereals.

mean: _____   median: _____

mode: _____   range: _____

What Is in Your Cereal Box? *(cont.)*

g. For each kind of cereal, record the amount of dietary fiber in one serving.

Name of Cereal	Dietary Fiber

h. Create a stem-and-leaf plot for the dietary fiber in each cereal.

i. Calculate the mean, median, mode, and range for the dietary fiber.

mean: _____   **median:** _____

mode: _____   **range:** _____

j. For each kind of cereal, record the amount of sugar in one serving.

Name of Cereal	Sugar

k. Create a stem-and-leaf plot for the sugars in each cereal.

l. Find the mean, median, mode, and range for the sugars.

mean: _____   **median:** _____

mode: _____   **range:** _____

#50026—Graphing Calculator Strategies, Middle School Math   © *Shell Education*

Experimenting with Probability

Analyzing Data

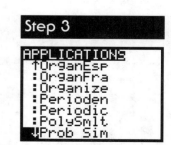

Lesson Description

- The students will represent all possible outcomes for compound events in an organized way and express the theoretical probability of each outcome.
- The students will use experimental probability to determine if a game is fair.

Materials

- *Practice! Practice! Probability* (page 107; data107.pdf)
- *Fair or Not?* (pages 108–109; data108.pdf)
- *SPIN-O Game* (page 110; data110.pdf)
- TI-83/84 Plus Family Graphing Calculator or TI-73 Explorer™

Explaining the Concept/Using the Calculator

Step 1

Ask students the following questions:

- What is theoretical probability? *Answer: A statement of probability on the chance that an event will occur. It is the number of favorable outcomes out of the number of possible outcomes.*
- What is experimental probability? *Answer: A statement of probability on the results of a series of trials*

Step 2

Have students find the theoretical probability for the following scenarios:

- A tossed coin landing on heads
- Rolling a one on a six-sided die
- On a spinner divided into four equal parts, landing on the number three

Step 3

Turn on the Probability Simulation on the graphing calculator.

- Press **APPS**. Use the down arrow to scroll down and highlight **Prob Sim** for the **probability simulation**. Then press **ENTER**.
- To start the simulator, press any key. To move from each screen, use the arrow keys at the top of the graphing calculator.

> **Step 3**
>
> APPLICATIONS
> ↑OrganEsp
> :OrganFra
> :Organize
> :Perioden
> :Periodic
> :PolySmlt
> ↓Prob Sim

Experimenting with Probability *(cont.)*

Analyzing Data

Explaining the Concept/Using the Calculator *(cont.)*

Step 4   Show students how to use the Toss Coins feature.

- Press [1] to select **TOSS COINS**.

- Press the **TOSS** soft key or [WINDOW] to flip the coin. The **T** represents tails and the **H** represents heads.

- Press the **CLEAR** soft key or [GRAPH]. Select the **YES** soft key or [Y=] to clear all trials.

Steps 4, 6, 7

Step 5   Have students find the experimental probability of landing on tails in 10 trials.

- Press the **+10** soft key or [ZOOM] to flip the coin ten times.

- Press the right arrow to find the frequency for heads and tails.

- This example shows the experimental probability for tails is 4/10.

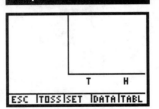

Step 4

Step 6   Find the experimental probability of rolling a one on a six-sided die in 10 trials.

- Press **ESC** soft key or [Y=] several times to return to the simulaton menu. Press [2] to select **Roll Dice**.

- Press the **SET** soft key or [ZOOM] to access the Settings editor.

- Move the cursor to **Trial Set** and input **10**. Press the **OK** soft key or [GRAPH].

- Press the **ROLL** soft key or [WINDOW].

- The example on the right shows that the experimental probability for rolling a one is 3/10.

- Use the right cursor to find the frequency.

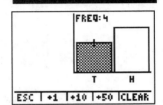

Step 5

Step 6

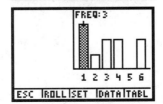

Step 6 *(cont.)*

Experimenting with Probability *(cont.)*

Analyzing Data

Explaining the Concept/Using the Calculator *(cont.)*

Step 7

Find the experimental probability of landing on the number three, using a spinner that is divided into four equal parts.

- Press **ESC** soft key or [Y=] several times to return to the simulation menu. Press [4], to select **Spin Spinner**.

- Press the **SET** soft key or [ZOOM] to access the Settings editor.

- Highlight **Trial Set** and input **10**. Highlight **Prob** to create a probability graph verses a frequency graph. Press the **OK** soft key or [GRAPH].

- Press the **SPIN** soft key or [WINDOW].

- The example on the right shows that the experimental probability for spinning a three is .2.

- Use the right cursor to find the probability in decimal form.

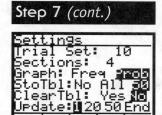

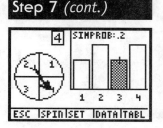

Step 8

Have students complete the activity sheet, *Practice! Practice! Probability* (page 107).

Applying the Concept

Step 1

Discuss the meaning of more and less likely or more and less probable. Write the following statements on the board:

- The greater the probability, the more likely the event is to occur.

- The lesser the probability, the less likely the event is to occur.

Step 2

Write the following "real-life" probability statements on the overhead or board:

- The probability of precipitation today is 80%.

- The chance of winning the lottery is 1 in 100,000.

- The chance of picking a red marble out of a bag of 10 marbles is 4 out of 10.

Experimenting with Probability *(cont.)*

Analyzing Data

Applying the Concept *(cont.)*

Step 3 | In groups, have the students discuss which event is more likely or less likely to occur and why. Have the groups share their findings with the class.

Step 4 | Have the groups create probability statements that would be more likely and less likely to occur.

- Have students write these statements on chart paper and share them with the class.

Step 5 | Have students complete the *Fair or Not?* (pages 108–109). Review the problems with the students.

Step 6 | Have students play the *SPIN–O Game* (page 110).

- Have students share any strategies they used when making up their game boards.

Extension Ideas

- Put students in small groups to create simple probability games and then calculate the theoretical probability of winning their games. Have groups exchange their games to play another group's game. Groups should calculate the theoretical probability of winning the games they are playing.

- Have students solve the following probability problem for a review or for homework.

  If all the numbers from 1 to 50 are written on golf balls and placed in a box, determine the probability of drawing a prime number.

- Using the Probability Simulation, have students determine the theoretical probability of picking marbles and drawing cards. Then have the students give the experimental probability.

Name _____

Date _____

Practice! Practice! Probability

Directions: Answer the questions below.

a. What is the **theoretical probability** of landing on heads and tails in a coin toss?

Heads: _____ **Tails:** _____

b. Use the Toss Coins on the Prob Sim App and flip the coin 300 times. Record the findings below.

Number of heads:	**Number of tails:**

c. What is the **experimental probability** of getting heads and tails?

Heads: _____ **Tails:** _____

d. When rolling a six-sided die, what is the **theoretical probability** of the following numbers?

1 _____ 2 _____ 3 _____

4 _____ 5 _____ 6 _____

e. Use Roll Dice on the Prob Sim App, to roll a dice 200 times. Record the **number of times** each number was rolled.

1:	2:	3:	4:	5:	6:

f. What was the **experimental probability** of rolling the following numbers?

1 _____ 2 _____ 3 _____

4 _____ 5 _____ 6 _____

g. Using a spinner divided into four equal parts and numbered 1–4, what is the **theoretical probability** of spinning the following numbers?

1 _____ 2 _____ 3 _____ 4 _____

h. Using the Spin Spinner feature, spin the spinner 400 times. Record the number of times the spinner landed on each number.

1:	2:	3:	4:

i. What was the **experimental probability** of spinning the following?

1 _____ 2 _____ 3 _____ 4 _____

j. Explain the difference between **experimental** and **theoretical probability**.

_____

Name _____

Date _____

Fair or Not?

Directions: The students at Kent Middle School are having a Spring Carnival. Below are some of the games the students will be able to play. Answer the questions on a separate piece of paper to determine in which booths a player has the least or greatest probability of scoring a point.

Booth 1	**Booth 4**
Toss a coin. Landing on heads will score 1 point.	Roll 2 six-sided cubes. Calculate the sum of the 2 digits. Rolling a sum of 2, 7, or 12 will score 1 point.
Booth 2	**Booth 5**
Roll a 6-sided cube. Rolling a 2 or a 4 will score 1 point.	Roll 2 six-sided cubes. Calculate the sum of the 2 digits. Rolling a sum of 4, 8, or 10 will score 1 point.
Booth 3	**Booth 6**
Roll a 6-sided cube. Rolling a 1, 3, or 5 will score 1 point.	Spin a spinner with four equal parts that are numbered 1–4. Landing on a 2 will score 1 point.

a. In which booth is a player most likely to score a point? Explain why.

_____

_____

b. In which booth is a player least likely to score a point? Explain why.

_____

_____

c. With a partner, play each game using the graphing calculator. How many points did you earn? Would you change your choice of the booths with the greatest and least probability of scoring points? Explain why or why not.

_____

_____

d. Now play each game again, but this time, use 10 trials. Record the number of tosses, rolls, and spins in the tables on the following page.

Name _____

Date _____

Fair or Not? *(cont.)*

Booth 1	
Number of Heads	
Number of Tails	
Total Tosses	

Booth 2	
2s rolled	
4s rolled	
Total Rolls	

Booth 3	
1s rolled	
3s rolled	
5s rolled	
Total Rolls	

Booth 4	
Sums of 2 rolled	
Sums of 7 rolled	
Sums of 12 rolled	
Total rolls	

Booth 5	
Sums of 4 rolled	
Sums of 8 rolled	
Sums of 10 rolled	
Total rolls	

Booth 6	
Spins on 2	
Total Spins	

Directions: Answer the questions below to explain your findings.

e. Compare the outcomes of playing your games with those of your classmates. How are your outcomes similar or different?

_____

_____

f. In which booth is it least likely to score a point? How could you change the game to make it more likely for players to score a point?

_____

_____

g. Design a new booth using coins, cubes, and/or spinners. Describe how to play the game in your booth and explain the theoretical probabilities for the outcomes.

_____

_____

Name _____

Date _____

SPIN-O Game

Directions: Determine the theoretical probability of the spinner used in the game SPIN-O and then play the game as instructed below.

a. Using a spinner divided into 4 equal parts and numbered 1–4, determine the theoretical probability of spinning the following numbers.

        1 _____   **2** _____

        3 _____   **4** _____

b. Place a number 1–4 in each square of the game board below. Take turns with a partner to spin the spinner in the Probability Simulation application on the graphing calculator. Place a counter over the number on the game card that appears on the spinner. The person who covers the entire game board first wins the game.

SPIN–O Game Board

S	P	I	N	O

c. Now change the weight of each number. What is the theoretical probability of spinning the following numbers.

        1 _____   **2** _____

        3 _____   **4** _____

d. Is this game fair? Why or why not?

_____

_____

e. What would the spinner need to look like for your game board to have a better chance to win?

_____

_____

Constructing Box-and-Whisker Plots

Analyzing Data

Lesson Description

- Students will be able to define and compute the minimum, the lower quartile, the median, the upper quartile, and the maximum of a set of data.
- Students will create a box-and-whisker plot for a given set of data.

Materials

- *Practice! Practice! Box-and-Whisker Plot* (page 114; data114.pdf)
- *NFL Games* (pages 115–116; data115.pdf)
- *More Box-and-Whisker Plots* (page 117–118; data117.pdf)
- TI-83/84 Plus Family Graphing Calculator or TI-73 Explorer™

Explaining the Concept

Step 1   Ask students the following question:
- *What is a box-and-whisker plot? Answer: A graph that uses a rectangle to represent the middle 50% of a data set and uses whiskers at the ends of the rectangle to represent the bottom 25% and top 25% of a data set.*

Step 2   Read the following scenario and write the data on the board:
The tourist bureau of the city that is the "Family Recreation Capital of the World," has collected the following data on the cost of adult admission for a random sample of theme parks and recreation venues. The tourist bureau needs to create a box-and-whisker plot of the data for the brochures that they send to potential visitors.

$54, $91, $61, $100, $18, $85, $34, $82, $78, $59, $68, $93, $27, $52, $87

Step 3   Have the students write the data in numerical order in their notes, as shown below.

• **18, 27, 34,** │ **52, 54, 59, 61, 68, 78, 82, 85, 87,** │ **91, 93, 100** •

Lower Quartile   Upper Quartile

Step 4   Have students calculate the median of the above data. Then draw a box around the number. *Answer: The median is 68.*

Step 5   Have students calculate the median of the numbers to the left of the line and draw a line before the number. *Answer: The median is 52.* This number is the lower quartile.

Step 6   Have students find the median of the numbers to the right of the line and draw a line after the number. *Answer: 87.* This number is the upper quartile.

Constructing Box-and-Whisker Plots *(cont.)*

Analyzing Data

Explaining the Concept *(cont.)*

Step 7 | Have students create a box around the lower and upper quartiles.

- Have students draw a dot by the smallest number, which is the **lower extreme**, and a dot by the largest number, which is the **upper extreme**.

- Have students draw a line from the smallest number to the lower quartile, and a line from the largest number to the upper quartile.

- The diagram below shows the box-and-whisker plot that has been created.

18 27 34 | 52 54 59 61 68 78 82 85 87 | 91 93 100

Step 8 | If necessary, repeat this activity using student-generated data.

Using the Calculator

Step 1 | Have students use the data from the **Explaining the Concept Section** to create a box-and-whisker plot on the graphing calculator.

- Access the Stat List editor by pressing **STAT** and then **ENTER**. Input the data below into **L1** by typing a number and pressing **ENTER**.

> **54, 91, 61, 100, 18, 85, 34, 82, 78, 59, 68, 93, 27, 52, 87**

Step 2 | Have students select the settings for the box-and-whisker plot.

- Press **2ND** and then **Y=** to access the Stat Plot editor. Press **ENTER** to access **Plot1**.

- Select the following settings by highlighting them and pressing **ENTER**. Turn on Plot1; by **Type**, select the fifth icon (the second box-and-whisker plot). Then by **Xlist**, input **L1** (**2ND**, **1**) and by **Freq**, press **1**.

Step 3 | Have students view and analyze the plot in an appropriate window.

- Press **ZOOM** and then **9** to view the graph in a **ZoomStat** window.

- Press **TRACE**. Use the right and left arrow keys to move along the plot.

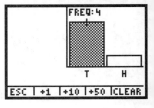

Constructing Box-and-Whisker Plots *(cont.)*

Analyzing Data

Using the Calculator *(cont.)*

Step 4   Have students complete the activity sheet, *Practice! Practice! Box-and-Whisker Plot* (page 114). Review the problems with the students.

Applying the Concept

Step 1   Discuss the components of a box-and-whisker plot. Ask students when a box-and-whisker plot is used versus other types of graphs.

Step 2   Write the following scenarios on the overhead or board:

> - Jack wants to graph the time he spends reading each day.
>   *Recommended graph: line graph or bar graph*
>
> - Mrs. Smith wants to find the average test score of her math class.
>   *Recommended graph: box-and-whisker plot*
>
> - Sue wants to find the percentages of people working in various occupations in her community.
>   *Recommended graph: circle graph*
>
> - Mr. Holiday wants to display his students' heights.
>   *Recommended graph: stem-and-leaf plot*

Step 3   Have students share with a partner or small group which graph they would use for each scenario.
- Have them record their conclusions on a separate piece of paper and explain why they believe that graph will best represent the data generated.

Step 4   Have students complete *NFL Games* (pages 115–116).

Step 5   Have students complete the activity sheet, *More Box-and-Whisker Plots* (pages 117–118).
- Review the problems with the students.

Extension Idea
- Look through a newspaper and/or magazine to locate data to create a box-and-whisker plot.

Name _____

Date _____

Practice! Practice! Box-and-Whisker Plot

Directions: Use the data below to create a box-and-whisker plot on the graphing calculator.

Major League Base-Running Times in Seconds

3.8, 3.2, 2.8, 4.9, 4.3, 4.1, 6.5, 4.0, 4.1, 4.4,

4.5, 5.0, 4.9, 4.0, 4.7, 4.6, 2.9, 5.3, 5.5, 4.2

a. Draw the box-and-whisker plot shown on the graphing calculator below.

b. Use the box-and-whisker plot to calculate the following.

mean _____   lower quartile _____

median _____   upper extreme _____

upper quartile _____   lower extreme _____

Directions: Use the data below to create a box-and-whisker plot on the graphing calculator.

Combined Scores from the First Forty Super Bowls

45, 47, 23, 30, 29, 27, 21, 31, 22, 38, 46, 37, 66, 50, 37, 47, 44, 47, 54, 56,

59, 52, 36, 65, 39, 61, 69, 43, 75, 44, 56, 55, 53, 39, 41, 37, 69, 61, 45, 31

c. Draw the box-and-whisker plot shown on the graphing calculator below.

d. Use the box-and-whisker plot to calculate the following.

mean _____   lower quartile _____

median _____   upper extreme _____

upper quartile _____   lower extreme _____

e. Based on the data collected, predict the combined score of the next Super Bowl. Explain.

_____

_____

Name _____

Date _____

NFL Games

Directions: Imagine that you get to attend 17 National Football League (NFL) games. In the table on page 116, record 17 NFL teams that you would like to see. Use the table below to find the location of each stadium. Calculate the number of miles you will travel from your hometown to each of your chosen NFL stadiums. Once all the data has been recorded, create a box-and-whisker plot.

Team	Location	Team	Location
Baltimore Ravens	Baltimore, MD	Arizona Cardinals	Glendale, AZ
Buffalo Bills	Orchard Park, NY	Atlanta Falcons	Atlanta, GA
Cincinnati Bengals	Cincinnati, OH	Carolina Panthers	Charlotte, NC
Cleveland Browns	Cleveland, OH	Chicago Bears	Chicago, IL
Denver Broncos	Denver, CO	Dallas Cowboys	Irving, TX
Houston Texans	Houston, TX	Detroit Lions	Detroit, MI
Indianapolis Colts	Indianapolis, IN	Green Bay Packers	Green Bay, WI
Jacksonville Jaguars	Jacksonville, FL	Minnesota Vikings	Minneapolis, MN
Kansas City Chiefs	Kansas City, MO	New Orleans Saints	New Orleans, LA
Miami Dolphins	Miami, FL	New York Giants	E. Rutherford, NJ
New England Patriots	Foxboro, MA	Philadelphia Eagles	Philadelphia, PA
New York Jets	E. Rutherford, NJ	San Francisco 49ers	San Francisco, CA
Oakland Raiders	Oakland, CA	Seattle Seahawks	Seattle, WA
Pittsburgh Steelers	Pittsburgh, PA	St. Louis Rams	St. Louis, MO
San Diego Chargers	San Diego, CA	Tampa Bay Buccaneers	Tampa, FL
Tennessee Titans	Nashville, TN	Washington Redskins	Raljon, MD

Name _____

Date _____

NFL Games *(cont.)*

Team	Location	Miles Traveled

Team	Location	Miles Traveled

a. Create a box-and-whisker plot on the graphing calculator. Then draw your plot in the box below.

b. Calculate the following statistics using the data and the box-and-whisker plot above.

mean _____   lower quartile _____

median _____   upper extreme _____

upper quartile _____   lower extreme _____

c. Compare your results with a partner. Who traveled the greatest and least number of miles? Make two other comparisons about your data.

_____

_____

_____

More Box-and-Whisker Plots

Directions: Use the data given below to create a box-and-whisker plot and to calculate the statistics.

I. Kamryn's mom brought home some gladiola plants to plant in her garden. Kamryn read the information tag on the plants and discovered that they can grow up to 1 1/2 feet tall. She decided to keep a record of the plants' heights until they reached 30 inches. The stem-and-leaf plot shows her findings.

Tens	Ones
1	7, 7, 7, 9
2	0, 1, 1, 1, 3, 3, 5, 7, 7, 8, 8, 9, 9, 9
3	0

a. Use the data above to create a box-and-whisker plot on the graphing calculator. Draw the plot in the box below.

b. Calculate the following statistics using the box-and-whisker plot above.

mean _____   lower quartile _____

median _____   upper extreme _____

upper quartile _____   lower extreme _____

More Box-and-Whisker Plots *(cont.)*

Cooperative Group Activity

II. Give the last digit of your telephone number to each of your classmates. Use the table below to record the data. Create a box-and-whisker plot to display the data.

Digit	Tally	Total
0		
1		
2		
3		
4		
5		
6		
7		
8		
9		

c. Draw the box-and-whisker plot shown on the graphing calculator in the box below.

d. Calculate the following statistics using the data and the box-and-whisker plot above.

mean _____   lower quartile _____

median _____   upper extreme _____

upper quartile _____   lower extreme _____

Making Circle Graphs

Analyzing Data

Lesson Description

- Students will organize and display single-variable data in appropriate multiple representations, such as graphs and tables.
- Students will create a circle graph for a given set of data.

Materials

- *Practice! Practice! Circle Graphs* (pages 123–124; data123.pdf)
- *Survey Says* (page 125; data125.pdf)
- *How Do You Spend Your Day?* (page 126; data126.pdf)
- TI-83/84 Plus Family Graphing Calculator or TI-73 Explorer™

Explaining the Concept

Step 1

Ask students the following question:

- What is a circle graph? *Answer: A graph that is used to show how parts, usually expressed as percentages, make up a whole.*

Step 2

As a class, read the activity sheet, *Practice! Practice! Circle Graphs* (pages 123–124). Below is the completed table.

- Complete **Part I** by creating a circle graph using a fraction bar and then calculating the fraction, decimal, and percent for each section of the graph.
- Then answer question C.

Category	$ Per Month	Fraction	Decimal	Percent
Clothes	$16.00	16/40 = 2/5	.40	40%
Music	$6.00	6/40 = 3/20	.15	15%
Movies	$4.00	4/40 = 1/10	.10	10%
Savings	$12.00	12/40 = 3/10	.30	30%
Miscellaneous	$2.00	2/40 = 1/20	.05	5%

Making Circle Graphs *(cont.)*

Analyzing Data

Using the Calculator

Step 1 Have students use the CelSheet application on the graphing calculator to create a circle graph of the earnings distribution from Part I of *Practice! Practice! Circle Graphs* (pages 123-124).

- To access the CelSheet application, press **APPS** and scroll down until **CelSheet** is highlighted. Then press **ENTER** twice until the spreadsheet appears on the screen.

Step 2 Enter the text into column A on the cell sheet. Any character string that is preceded by quotation marks is treated as text.

- For example, to enter **"clothes,"** press **ALPHA** and then **+** to access the quotation marks.

- To turn on Alpha Lock (A-Lock), press **ALPHA** and then press the keys for the corresponding letters, which appear in green above the key. The necessary keystrokes for the word **"clothes"** are shown below.

PGRM , **)** , **7** , **4** , **^** , **SIN** , **LN** .

- Press **ENTER** to input the word in the cell.

- If you make a mistake in typing a character, highlight the word in the cell, press **ENTER**, and then highlight the character in the word and press **DEL** to delete the character or press **2ND** and then **DEL** to insert a character.

- Repeat the steps above to input the other categories, **"savings," "movies," "music,"** and **"misc."**

Step 3 Input the percentages from the table on page 119 in column B of the cell sheet.

- Highlight each cell in column B, type the percentage, and press **ENTER**.

Making Circle Graphs *(cont.)*

Analyzing Data

Using the Calculator *(cont.)*

Step 4   Have students select the settings for the Pie chart (circle graph).

- Press the **Menu** soft key or **GRAPH** to access the **CELLSHEET MENU**.

- Press **4** to select **Charts** and access the **CHARTS** menu. Press **7** to select Pie.

- On the **PIE CHART** menu by **Categories** input the cell range **A1:A5** by pressing **ALPHA**, **MATH**, **1**, **ALPHA**, **.**, **ALPHA**, **MATH**, **5**.

- By **Series**, input the cell range **B1:B5** by pressing **ALPHA**, **APPS**, **1** **ALPHA**, **.**, **ALPHA** **APPS**, **5**.

- Below **Series**, select **Percent** by highlighting and pressing **ENTER**.

- By **Title**, input the text **"Earnings"** by pressing the **ALPHA** and then the key of the corresponding letter.

Step 5   To view the pie chart (circle graph) that shows the percentages of the distribution of the earnings, highlight **Draw** and then press **ENTER**.

- Press **TRACE** to see the percentage for each category. Use the down cursor to view the other percentages.

Step 6   Have students compare their answers to those on the activity sheet, *Practice! Practice! Circle Graphs* (pages 123–124).

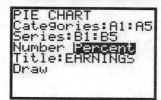

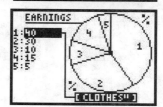

Making Circle Graphs *(cont.)*

Analyzing Data

Using the Calculator *(cont.)*

Step 7   Have students complete **Part II** of the activity sheet, *Practice! Practice! Circle Graphs* (page 124).

• Review the problems with students.

Applying the Concept

Step 1   Ask students when a circle graph is used versus other types of graphs. *Answer: Circle graphs are used for comparing parts of a whole.*

Step 2   As a class, have students give scenarios in which data would be generated to create a circle graph. Record this data on the overhead or board.

Step 3   Have students complete the activity sheet, *Survey Says* (page 125).

• Place students in small groups and assign each group a graph to present on chart paper. Have students draw the circle graph on the chart paper.

• Display the circle graphs around the room. Have students walk around the room writing statements or questions that analyze the data displayed in the circle graphs.

Step 4   Have students complete the activity sheet, *How Do You Spend Your Day?* (page 126).

Extension Ideas

• Have students gather data on a topic of their choice. Students should create a table to organize their data and then create a circle graph on the graphing calculator.

• Have students look through a newspaper or magazines for circle graphs. Have students write mathematical statements analyzing the data presented in the graph.

Name _____

Date _____

Practice! Practice! Circle Graphs

Directions: Create a circle graph and answer the questions below.

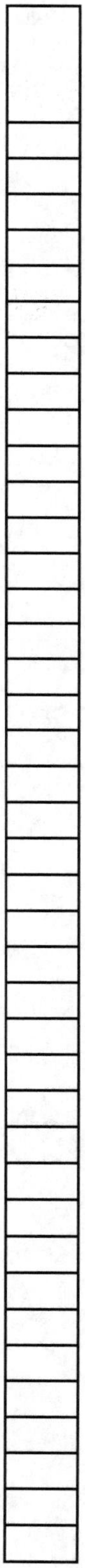

I.   You earn $40 a month by doing odd jobs around your house. The table below shows how your earnings are distributed among the items you purchase.

a. Create a circle graph of the data. Use the bar on the side of the activity sheet to create sections of the graph that are proportional to the amount of money spent. There are a total of 40 sections on the bar, each representing one dollar. Shade the number of dollars spent in each category with a different color. Cut the bar out and place it around the circle graph. Draw a line where each category begins and ends. Then label the circle graph.

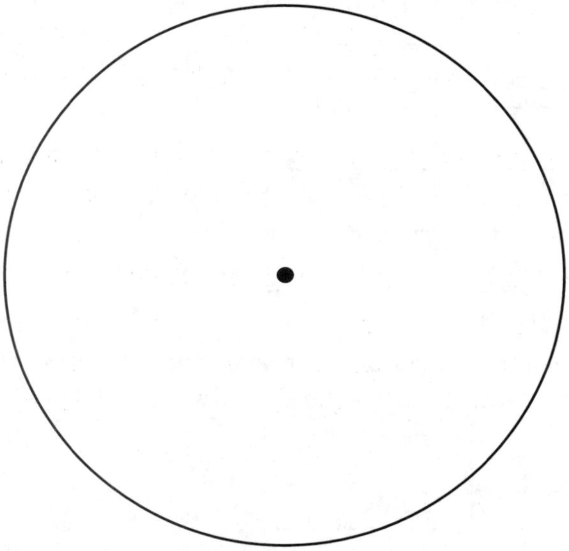

b. Calculate the fraction, decimal, and percent for the amount of money designated in each category. Write the percents on the circle graph above.

Category	$ Per Month	Fraction	Decimal	Percent
Clothes	$16.00			
Music	$6.00			
Movies	$4.00			
Savings	$12.00			
Miscellaneous	$2.00			

c. Based on the data in the circle graph above, if you made $200 in a month, how much would you spend in each of the following categories?

   clothes _____   **music** _____   **movies** _____

   savings _____   **misc.** _____

Practice! Practice! Circle Graphs *(cont.)*

II. The table below shows the number of students at Huntsville Middle School who participate in Saturday sports.

d. Sketch the circle graph from the graphing calculator. Write the percent for each sport.

Sport	Number of Students	Percent
Baseball	35	
Gymnastics	5	
Tennis	15	
Soccer	60	
Swimming	25	
Basketball	50	

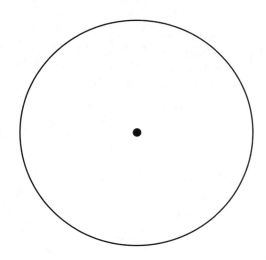

e. The table below shows the percentages of 7th grade students who saw the school play each day of the week. Sketch the circle graph from the graphing calculator.

Day of the Week	Percent	Number of Students
Monday	18.75%	
Tuesday	12.5%	
Wednesday	18.75%	
Thursday	21.875%	
Friday	28.125%	

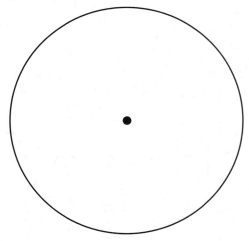

f. If 320 students were surveyed, how many students saw the school play for each day of the week? Record your answer in the table above.

Name

Date

Survey Says

Directions: Collect data by surveying 20 people. Create a circle graph on the graphing calculator and sketch it in the box next to the table.

a. What is your favorite extreme sport?

Sport	Tally
Rock Climbing	
Mountain Biking	
Surfing	
Snowboarding	

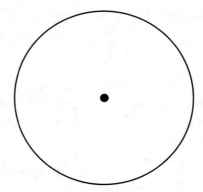

b. Which electronic device do you use most often to listen to music?

Electronic Device	Tally
MP3 player	
CD player	
Radio	
Computer	

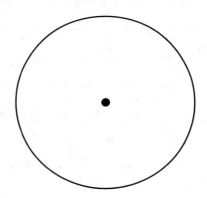

c. Who influences your opinions the most?

People	Tally
Parents	
Friends	
Celebrities	
Teachers	
Media	
Other	

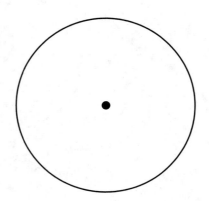

Name _____

Date _____

How Do You Spend Your Day?

Directions: How do you spend your day from the time you wake up until the time you go to sleep? Record how much time you spend doing each activity and then create a circle graph of the activities.

a. At what time do you usually wake up? _____

b. At what time do you usually go to sleep? _____

c. Approximately how many minutes are there between the time you wake up and the time you go to sleep? _____

d. Use the table to record the activities you do in a day, such as eating, getting dressed, and doing homework. Then determine the number of minutes you spend doing each activity. Write these as fractions by writing the number of minutes spent doing each activity out of the number of minutes that you are awake.

Activity	Total Minutes	Fraction	Percent

e. Sketch a circle graph of the distribution of activities that you do during the day.

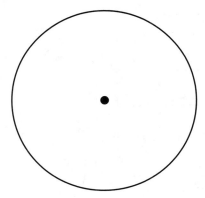

f. What do you spend most of your time doing?

_____

g. What do you spend the least amount of time doing?

_____

Developing Spatial Reasoning

Developing Spatial Reasoning

#50026—*Graphing Calculator Strategies, Middle School Math*

© *Shell Education*

Plotting Shapes on the Coordinate Plane

Developing Spatial Reasoning

Lesson Description

- Students will graph ordered pairs in the four quadrants of a coordinate plane.
- Students will plot points on a coordinate plane to form a geometric shape. Then they will calculate the area and perimeter of the shape.

Materials

- **Appendix C:** *Small Coordinate Planes* (page 204; appnd204.pdf)
- *Practice! Practice! Coordinate Planes* (page 132; sptl132.pdf)
- *Plotting Points* (page 133; sptl133.pdf)
- *How Many Shapes?* (page 134; sptl134.pdf)
- TI-83/84 Plus Family Graphing Calculator or TI-73 Explorer™

Explaining the Concept

Step 1   Ask students the following question:

- Why do city maps use a letter and number grid to identify locations?
  Answer: To help people quickly find and remember locations on the map

Step 2   On the *Small Coordinate Planes* template in Appendix C (page 204), have students plot the following points, (6, 9) (–5, 9) (–5, –4) (6, –4).

- Explain how to plot the points with the students. The first number in the pair is the *x*-coordinate, or the horizontal axis. The second number is the *y*-coordinate, or the vertical axis.

Step 3   Have students connect the points. Ask the students what type of shape is formed. *Answer: Rectangle*

Step 4   Have students find the area and perimeter of the rectangle. *Answer: Area: 11 times 13 = 143 square units. Perimeter: 2(11) + 2(11) = 48 units*

Step 5   Using a second coordinate grid on the *Small Coordinate Planes* template, have the students plot the ordered pair, (3, 5).

- From that point, tell students to move 5 units to the left and 2 units down. Have students plot the point and write the ordered pair, (–2, 3). Check for understanding.
- From that point, have students move 7 units right and 6 units up. Have students plot the point and write the ordered pair, (5, 9). Check for understanding.

Step 6   Have students complete the activity, *Practice! Practice! Coordinate Planes* (page 132).

Plotting Shapes on the Coordinate Plane *(cont.)*

Developing Spatial Reasoning

Using the Calculator

Step 1 Plot the ordered pairs, (6, 9) (–5, 9) (–5, –4) (6, –4) on the graphing calculator.

- Press **STAT** and then **ENTER** to access the Stat List editor.

- Input the *x*-coordinates in **L1** and the *y*-coordinates in **L2**. Highlight the place in the column, type the coordinate, and press **ENTER**.

Step 2 Set up a scatter plot to display the coordinates.

- Press **Y=** and **CLEAR** all graphs.

- Press **2ND** and then **Y=** to access the Stat Plot editor. Then press **1** to select Plot 1.

- Select the following settings by highlighting each and pressing **ENTER**. Turn **On** the plot. By **Type**, select the scatter plot, which is the first icon. By **Xlist**, input **L1** (**2ND**, **1**). By **YList**, input **L2** (**2ND**, **2**). By **Mark**, select the first icon.

Step 3 Have students view the points on a grid.

- Press **2ND** and then **ZOOM**. Move the cursor to highlight **GridOn** and press **ENTER** to select it.

- Access **ZStandard** window by pressing **ZOOM** and then **6**.

Step 4 Have students connect the points of the scatter plot.

- Press **STAT** and then **ENTER** to access the Stat List editor.

- Keep the ordered pairs in L1 and L2, but add the first ordered pair (6, 9) to the end of the list.

- When connecting points, students must think about it as using a pencil to trace from a starting point through the other points and then back to the starting point. *(See the screen shot on page 131.)*

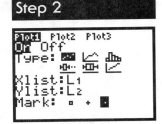

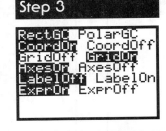

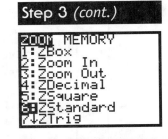

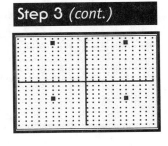

Plotting Shapes on the Coordinate Plane *(cont.)*

Develop Spatial Reasoning

Using the Calculator *(cont.)*

Step 5

Have students create a line graph to connect the points.

- Press **2ND** and then **Y=** to access the Stat Plot editor and return to Plot 1. Instead of selecting the scatter plot (first icon), select the line graph (second icon).

- Press **GRAPH** to view the scatter plot.

Step 6

Have students complete the activity sheet, *Plotting Points* (page 133).

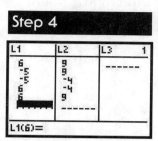

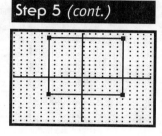

Applying the Concept

Step 1

Position the desks in rows to create a real-life coordinate grid. Use yarn or string to label the *x*- and *y*-axis.

Step 2

Have the students represent points on the real-life coordinate grid.

- Have each student on the grid give his/her ordered pair.

- Give directions, such as, "If Brita moved 2 units to the right and 3 units up, where would she be?"

- Ask a student volunteer to state the new ordered pair. Then have the student move to check if the given ordered pair is correct.

- Repeat the activity with other students.

Step 3

Have students complete the activity sheet, *How Many Shapes?* (page 134). Review the problems with students.

Extension Ideas

- To enhance mental math skills, give students an ordered pair, such as (5, 6) and have them tell in which quadrant it is located.

- Have students play Win, Lose, or Draw on the overhead. Write a series of coordinate pairs on a note card. Have a student plot the points on a coordinate plane that is displayed on the overhead. As students are plotting the points, they should guess what picture the coordinate pairs will form.

Practice! Practice! Coordinate Planes

Directions: Follow the directions for the problems below.

I. Plot the points on the coordinate grid and then use the graphing calculator to check them.

a. (6, –3) (–5, –4) (–2, 5) (1, 5)

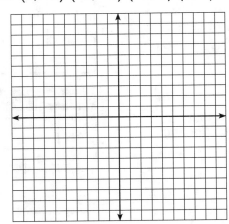

b. (–1, –5) (4, 2) (3, –4) (–6, 3)

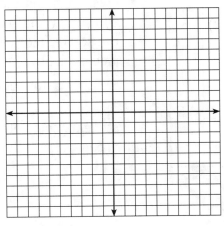

II. Using the starting point and coordinate plane, plot the next three points on the graphing calculator. Write the ordered pairs in the table below.

X	Y	
–2	–4	Starting point—move 6 units to the right 3 units up
		2 units to the left 5 units down
		7 units to the left 3 units up
		Ending point

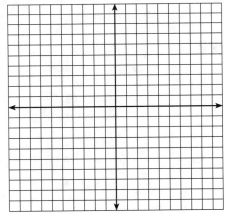

III. Graph the points on the graphing calculator and below. Then calculate the area and perimeter.

X	Y
–2	3
–2	–3
3	–3
3	3
–2	3

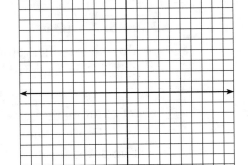

c. Area = _____

d. Perimeter = _____

Name _____

Date _____

Plotting Points

Directions: For each problem, input the ordered pairs in L1 and L2 of the Stat List editor on the graphing calculator. Set up a line graph in the Stat Plot editor and plot the points on a coordinate grid. Then calculate the area and perimeter of each shape. Remember to clear L1 and L2 after each problem.

a. (5, 2) (–5, 2) (–5, –3), (5, –3) (5, 2)

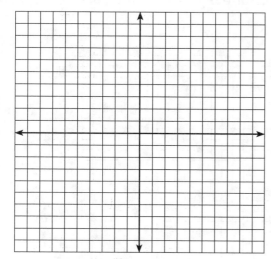

Area = _____   Perimeter = _____

b. (4, 4) (–4, –3) (4, –3) (4, 4)

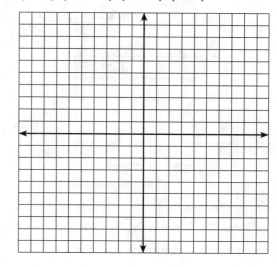

Area = _____   Perimeter = _____

c. (–2, 1) (–6, –3) (6, –3) (2, 1) (–2, 1)

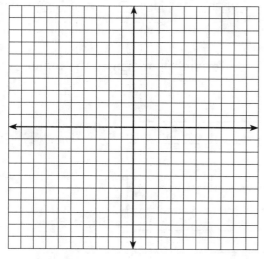

Area = _____   Perimeter = _____

d. (–5, 5) (–5, –5) (5, –5) (5, 5) (–5, 5)

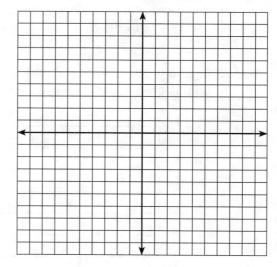

Area = _____   Perimeter = _____

e. On a separate sheet of paper explain how you calculated the perimeter and area for the shapes.

Name _____

Date _____

How Many Shapes?

Directions: Follow the steps below.

I. Create the shape shown in the coordinate plane below on the graphing calculator.

    a. Write the ordered pairs shown on the coordinate plane in the table below. Write the *x*-coordinates in L1 and the *y*-coordinates in L2.

    b. Input the points from the table into the L1 and L2 of the Stat List editor, and create a line graph in Plot 1 of the Stat Plot editor.

L1	L2

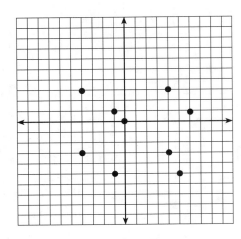

II. Create two new shapes, using some or all of the coordinate points listed in the table above.

    c. Input the coordinate points into L3, L4, L5, and L6 of the Stat List editor and then record them in the tables below.

    d. Create line graphs in Plots 2 and 3 of the Stat List editor and then display the graph. Plot the graphs on a separate piece of graph paper.

L3	L4

L5	L6

III. Find the approximate area and perimeter of all the shapes. Record it below the graphs. Did you create any smaller shapes by overlapping the others?

Transforming Figures on the Coordinate Plane

Developing Spatial Reasoning

Lesson Description

- Students will plot simple figures on coordinate graphs and determine how those images translate and reflect.

Materials

- **Appendix C:** *Grid Paper* (1/4 inch) (page 201; appnd201.pdf)
- **Appendix C:** *Pattern Blocks* (page 205; appnd205.pdf)
- *Practice! Practice! Transformations* (page 139; sptl139.pdf)
- *Transforming Shapes* (page 140; sptl140.pdf)
- *Rotations Game* (page 141; sptl141.pdf)
- TI-83/84 Plus Family Graphing Calculator or TI-73 Explorer™

Explaining the Concept

Step 1

Give each student a piece of *Grid Paper* (1/4 inch) (page 201) and a square pattern block to practice translating a shape on a coordinate plane.

- If pattern blocks are needed, use the template of *Pattern Blocks* (page 205).

- Instruct students to place the square on the coordinate plane and label the ordered pairs for the four corners of the square. Review the ordered pairs with the students.

- Have students move the square 4 units to the left and 2 units down. Have students label the ordered pairs for the four corners of the square. Review the ordered pairs with the students.

- From that point, have students move the square 7 units to the right and 5 units up. Have students label the ordered pairs for the four corners of the square. Review the ordered pairs with the students.

Step 2

Use the 1/4 inch grid paper and pattern blocks to practice reflecting a figure along the x- and y-axis.

- Have students create a figure from pattern blocks and trace it along the y-axis. Then, students should reflect the figure on the other side of the y-axis.

- Have students share the symmetry of their figures with classmates.

- Have students create another figure along the x-axis and then create the reflection of the figure along the x-axis.

Step 3

If needed, practice more translation and reflections with the students.

Transforming Figures on the Coordinate Plane *(cont.)*

Developing Spatial Reasoning

Using the Calculator

Step 1

Have students input the ordered pairs, (1, 4), (1, 1), (4, 1), (4, 4), (1, 4), into L1 and L2.

- Press **STAT** and then **ENTER** to access the Stat List editor.

- Input the *x*-coordinates in **L1** and the *y*-coordinates in **L2** by typing the coordinate and pressing **ENTER**.

  Special note: The coordinates must be entered clockwise or counterclockwise to connect the points with a line graph.

Step 2

Have students use the Stat Plot editor to create a line graph of the coordinate pairs.

- Press **2ND** and then **Y=** to access the Stat Plot editor. Then press **1** to select **Plot1**.

- Select the following settings by highlighting each and pressing **ENTER**. Turn **On** the plot. By **Type**, select the line graph, which is the second icon. By **Xlist**, input **L1** (**2ND**, **1**). By **Ylist**, input **L2** (**2ND**, **2**). By **Mark**, select the first icon (square dot).

Step 3

View the graph in an appropriate window and analyze the shape.

- Press **ZOOM** and ten **6** to set up a **ZStandard** window.

Step 4

Ask students, "If the square moved 4 units to the left and 3 units up, what would be the new coordinate points?" *Answer: (–3, 7), (–3, 4), (0, 4), (0, 7)*

- Model the following hint to figure out the new coordinate pairs. *Subtract from the x-coordinates if the figure is moving left. Add to the x-coordinates if the figure is moving right. Add to the y-coordinates if the figure is moving up. Subtract from the y-coordinates if the figure is moving down.*

Step 1

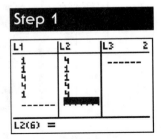

Step 2 & 9

Step 3

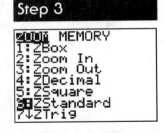

Step 4

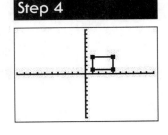

Transforming Figures on the Coordinate Plane (cont.)

Developing Spatial Reasoning

Using the Calculator (cont.)

Step 5   Have students repeat the steps above to input the new ordered pairs into **L3** and **L4**.

  • Remember to enter in the first coordinate pair twice to connect all the points.

Step 6   Instruct students to create a line graph in **Plot2** using **L3** for the **Xlist** and **L4** for the **Ylist**.

Step 7   Press [GRAPH] to view both squares.

  • Ask students if the movement of the square was a translation or reflection. *Answer: Translation*

Step 8   Have students repeat **Steps 1–3** above to input the ordered pairs, (2, 1), (7, 1), (7, 5), (2, 5), (2,1), into **L1** and **L2**.

Step 9   Instruct students to create a line graph in **Plot1** using **L1** for the **Xlist** and **L2** for the **Ylist**.

  • Remember to turn off **Plot2**.

Step 10   Ask students, "If the shape was reflected along the *x*-axis, what would the new ordered pairs be?"
Answer: (2, –1), (2, –5), (7, –5), (7, –1)

  • Have students input the new ordered pairs into **L3** and **L4**. Instruct students to create a line graph in **Plot2** using **L3** for the **Xlist** and **L4** for the **Ylist**.

Step 11   Have students complete the activity sheet, *Practice! Practice! Transformations* (page 139).

  • Have pairs of students present the problems. One student should present the problem on an overhead coordinate plane. The other student should present the problem on a projected graphing calculator.

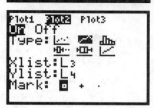

Steps 5 & 10

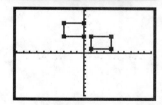

Step 6

Step 7

Steps 10

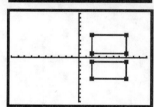

Step 10 (cont.)

Transforming Figures on the Coordinate Plane *(cont.)*

Developing Spatial Reasoning

Applying the Concept

Step 1　Have students look around the classroom, school building, or outside for examples of objects that have reflective symmetry.

Step 2　Give each student a piece of graph paper with the *x*- and *y*-axis drawn on it. Have each student draw one half of the reflection they observed on the paper.

Step 3　Have students trade papers with a partner and have them complete their partner's reflection.

Step 4　Have students write at least four coordinate points of their reflections, and two other mathematical statements about their reflections on the back of their graph papers.

Step 5　Display examples of students' reflections on the board or overhead.

- Test students' reflections by holding a mirror on the line of symmetry to see if the halves are the same.

- Ask students, "What geometric property do all of the reflection drawings have in common?" *Answer: Each drawing has a line of symmetry.*

Step 6　Have students complete the activity sheet, *Transforming Shapes* (page 140). Review the problems with the students.

Extension Ideas

- To enhance mental math skills, give the students an ordered pair such as (4,3). Ask students to give the new ordered pair if the point is moved 2 units to the left and 4 units down.

- Have students rotate shapes clockwise and counterclockwise, 45°, 90°, 180°, and 360°. Then have students create shapes on the graphing calculator and rotate them. Have students play the *Rotations Game* (page 141).

- Have students practice translations and rotations, using their bodies to either move side to side or turn around a specific number of degrees.

Practice! Practice! Transformations

Directions: Use the points to plot the triangles on a separate piece of graph paper and on the graphing calculator. Translate or reflect the triangle on the graph paper and on the graphing calculator. Record the ordered pairs in the tables below.

   a. Plot the points of the original triangle given in Table A.

   b. Translate the original triangle 5 units to the left and 3 units up and record the new coordinates in Table B.

   c. Translate the original triangle 3 units to the right and 4 units down and record the new coordinates in Table C.

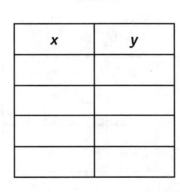

Table A

x	y
1	1
5	1
3	5
1	1

Table B

x	y

Table C

x	y

   d. Plot the points of the original triangle given in Table D.

   e. Reflect the original triangle along the *x*-axis and record the new coordinates in Table E.

   f. Reflect the original triangle along the *y*-axis and record the new coordinates in Table F.

Table D

x	y
1	1
3	3
1	5
1	1

Table E

x	y

Table F

x	y

Name _____

Date _____

Transforming Shapes

Directions: Follow the steps below to translate or reflect the shapes. Record all translations and reflections on a separate piece of graph paper or grid paper.

a. Plot a geometric shape in the third quadrant on the coordinate plane and on the graphing calculator. Record the ordered pairs in Table A.

b. Translate the original shape on the coordinate plane and on the graphing calculator 2 units to the left and 6 units up. Record the ordered pairs in Table B.

c. Translate the original shape on the coordinate plane and the graphing calculator 6 units to the right and 2 units down. Record the ordered pairs in Table C.

Table A		Table B		Table C	
x	*y*	*x*	*y*	*x*	*y*

d. Plot a geometric shape on the coordinate plane and on the graphing calculator. Record the ordered pairs in Table D.

e. Reflect the geometric shape along the *x*-axis on the coordinate plane and on the graphing calculator. Record the ordered pairs in Table E.

f. Reflect the geometric shape along the *y*-axis on the coordinate plane and on the graphing calculator. Record the ordered pairs in table F.

Table D		Table E		Table F	
x	*y*	*x*	*y*	*x*	*y*

Rotations Game

Directions: With a partner, follow the steps below to play the Rotation Game.

1. Partner 1 and partner 2 should individually create simple shapes on their graphing calculators.

   - Input the coordinates of the shape in L1 and L2 of the Stat List editor.
   - Create a line graph in the Plot1 in of the Stat Plot editor.

2. Partner 1 should give partner 2 the coordinate points to rotate the shape that was created on the graphing calculator.

   - Use the coordinate plane below to help visualize the coordinate points of the rotated shape.

3. Partner 2 should input the ordered pairs given by partner 1 into L3 and L4 in the graphing calculator.

4. Partner 2 should create a line graph of the shape in Plot2 of the Stat List editor.

5. Both partners should compare if a rotation of partner 1's shape was created on partner 2's calculator, and determine the number of degrees the shape was rotated.

6. Both partners should write two mathematical statements below about the figure that was rotated.

7. Repeat the game with partner 1 rotating the shape that partner 2 created on the calculator.

Degrees of Rotation: _____

Math Statements:

_____

_____

_____

_____

_____

Calculating Volume
Developing Spatial Reasoning

Lesson Description
- The students will understand the concept of volume and use the appropriate units to compute the volume of rectangular solids.
- The students will find the volume of rectangular prisms and cubes.

Materials
- *Practice! Practice! Volume* (pages 145; sptl145.pdf)
- *Voluminous Boxes* (page 147; sptl147.pdf)
- *Colored Cubes* (page 148; sptl148.pdf)
- TI-83/84 Plus Family Graphing Calculator or TI-73 Explorer™

Explaining the Concept/Using the Calculator

Step 1 Ask students the following questions:
- What is volume? *Answer: The number of cubic units it takes to fill a figure*
- How is volume measured? *Answer: Volume is measured in cubic units.*

Step 2 Give each student 20 linking cubes.
- Have students create a regular shape with a volume of 18.
- Have students share their shapes with the class by holding the shape in the air.
- Have students write the length, width, and height of their shapes.

Step 3 Show students how to calculate the volume of their rectangular prisms using the graphing calculator.
- Have a student share the length, width, and height of his/her shape. Write these values on the board or overhead, for example *w = 2, l = 3,* and *h = 3.*
- Multiply these values using the graphing calculator, by pressing [2], [×], [3], [×], [3]. Press [ENTER] to evaluate the expression.
- Ask students why all three values can be multiplied together without inserting parentheses or breaking the expression apart.
- *Refer to the screen shot on page 143.*

Calculating Volume *(cont.)*

Developing Spatial Reasoning

Explaining the Concept/Using the Calculator *(cont.)*

Step 4   Using 8 cubes, have students create a cube.

- Explain to students that a cube is a solid figure with six congruent square faces.

- Have students hold up their cubes. Ensure that students understand the characteristics of a cube.

- Have the students write the length, width, and height of their shapes.

Step 5   Working with a partner, have students use their cubes to determine which operation they would use to calculate dimensions of a cube if they knew the volume.

- Have them record their conclusions in their notes, and then discuss them.

Step 6   Show students how to use the graphing calculator to determine the sides of a cube when given the volume of 8.

- Press **MATH** to access the Math menu.

- Press **4** to select (the cube root symbol). Press **8** to input the volume.

- Press **)** to close the expression, and then press **ENTER** to evaluate the expression.

Step 7   Have students complete the activity sheet, *Practice! Practice! Volume* (pages 145–146). Review the problems with the students.

Step 8   Have students complete the activity sheet, *Voluminous Boxes* (page 147). Review the problems with the students.

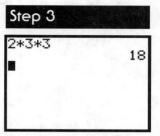

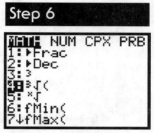

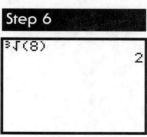

Calculating Volume *(cont.)*

Developing Spatial Reasoning

Applying the Concept

Step 1 Using cubes (linking or centimeter), hold up one and ask students how many faces the cube has. *Answer: Six*

Step 2 Place two cubes together to create a 2 by 1 by 1 rectangular prism. Tell students that the outside of the prism is painted. Ask the students how many faces are painted on each cube. *Answer: Five*

Step 3 Place four cubes together to create a 2 by 2 by 1 rectangular prism. Tell students that the prism is painted. Ask the students how many faces are painted on each cube. *Answer: Four*

Step 4 Have students complete the activity sheet, *Colored Cubes* (page 148). Review the problems with the students.

Extension Ideas

- Working in pairs or small groups, give students a box of sugar cubes. Have students determine how many shapes they can make using two cubes (1-domino), three cubes (2-trionimoes), four cubes (5-tetrominoes), five cubes (12-pentominoes).

- Have students investigate the perimeter and number of edges of these three-dimensional shapes. Students can create scatter plots of this data to see if any patterns emerge, e.g., number of cubes in the *x*-axis and number of edges in the *y*-axis.

Name _____

Date _____

Practice! Practice! Volume

Directions: Find the volume for each of the figures below.   Round all calculations to the nearest tenth.

a.

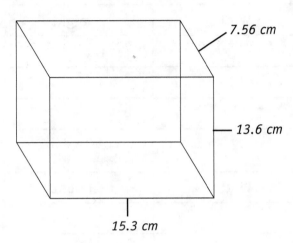

7.56 cm

13.6 cm

15.3 cm

Volume: _____

b.

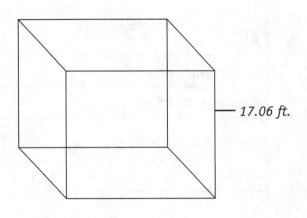

17.06 ft.

Volume: _____

c.

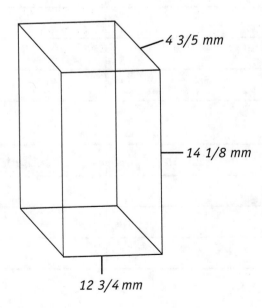

4 3/5 mm

14 1/8 mm

12 3/4 mm

Volume: _____

d.

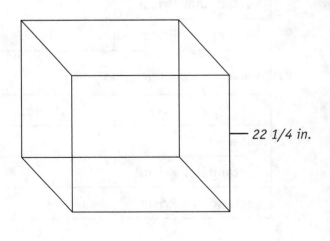

22 1/4 in.

Volume: _____

Name _____

Date _____

Practice! Practice! Volume *(cont.)*

Directions: Using the given volume, determine the dimensions of the cube and rectangular prisms. Record the length, width, and height of the cube and rectangular prisms in the table.

e. Volume: 64 cubic units

	Length	Width	Height
Cube			
Rectangular Prism			
Rectangular Prism			

f. Volume: 216 cubic units

	Length	Width	Height
Cube			
Rectangular Prism			
Rectangular Prism			

g. Volume: 729 cubic units

	Length	Width	Height
Cube			
Rectangular Prism			
Rectangular Prism			

h. Volume: 1,728 cubic units

	Length	Width	Height
Cube			
Rectangular Prism			
Rectangular Prism			

Name _____

Date _____

Voluminous Boxes

Directions: Work in a small group to solve the problems below. Use your graphing calculator to determine the volume.

I. Your team has been hired by a box-making company to reduce the waste that is created when they manufacture boxes. Create a lidless box from an 8½" x 11" piece of paper, so that it holds the greatest volume while wasting the least amount of material. Use the diagram below as a guide for making a lidless box out of the paper. Simply cut out the corners and fold up the sides. Calculate the volume of the box and the area of the wasted paper.

a. Volume: _____   **b. Wasted paper:** _____

II. Create a box that will hold 120 cubic centimeters. What is the length, width, and height?

c. Length: _____   **d. Width:** _____

e. Height: _____

III. Bring in a rectangular box from home. Measure the length, width, and height and record it below. Then calculate the volume of the box and write it on an index card.

f. Length: _____   **g. Width:** _____

h. Height: _____   **i. Volume:** _____

IV. Display the box and place the index card under the box. Work with your small group to estimate the volumes of the other boxes.

j. List your estimates with the corresponding box from least to greatest on the lines below. Then record your group's estimates on the board, listing the volumes from least to greatest.

_____

_____

k. Which group was closest to estimating the order of the boxes' volumes?

_____

Name _____

Date _____

Colored Cubes

Directions: Use small cubes to create larger cubes with the lengths given in the table below. Imagine the outside of each large cube is painted. Determine how many smaller cubes have three, two, one, and zero painted faces. Use the table to record your findings.

Length of Edge	Volume	Number of cubes with 3 painted faces	Number of cubes with 2 painted faces	Number of cubes with 1 painted face	Number of cubes with 0 painted faces
2					
3					
4					
5					
6					
N					

a. What patterns did you discover among the numbers in the table?

Directions: Use the information gathered in the table to answer the questions.

If the length of the edge is 20,

b. What is the volume? _____

c. What is the number of cubes with 3, 2, 1, and 0 painted faces?

   3 Faces: _____   2 Faces: _____

   1 Face: _____   0 Faces: _____

If the length of the edge is 32,

d. What is the volume? _____

e. What is the number of cubes with 3, 2, 1, and 0 painted faces?

   3 Faces: _____   2 Faces: _____

   1 Face: _____   0 Faces: _____

If the length of the edge is 55,

f. What is the volume? _____

g. What is the number of cubes with 3, 2, 1, and 0 painted faces?

   3 Faces: _____   2 Faces: _____

   1 Face: _____   0 Faces: _____

Tessellating with Regular & Irregular Shapes
Developing Spatial Reasoning

Lesson Description

- Students will analyze problems by identifying relationships and observing patterns.
- Students will discover which geometric shapes tessellate, then create a tessellation.

Materials

- **Appendix C:** *Regular Polygons* (page 207; appnd207.pdf)
- *Which Shapes Tessellate?* (page 153; sptl153.pdf)
- **Appendix C:** *Dot Paper* (page 208; appnd208.pdf)
- Copies of M.C. Escher's tessellations or pictures of tessellations
- *How to Make a Tessellating Shape* (pages 154–155; sptl154.pdf)
- TI-83/84 Plus Family Graphing Calculator or TI-73 Explorer™

Explaining the Concept

Step 1   Ask students the following questions:

- What are tessellations? *Answer: When a shape or combinations of shapes can completely cover a plane with no spaces and no overlaps*
- What is a regular polygon? *Answer: A convex polygon whose sides are all congruent and whose vertex angles are all congruent*

Step 2   Divide students into groups of three or four. Have students create patterns using the shapes on the template, *Regular Polygons* (page 207).

- Have students cut out the polygons on the template, *Regular Polygons*.
- Have students make their own patterns and sketch their designs on the *Dot Paper* (page 208).
- Encourage students to share their designs with their groups.

Step 3   Have students predict which shapes will tessellate.

- Students should record their predictions in the table on the activity sheet, *Which Shapes Tessellate?* (page 153).
- Each student should share his/her prediction with the others in the group. Then have each group share one prediction with the class. Write each group's predictions on the board or overhead.

Tessellating with Regular & Irregular Shapes *(cont.)*

Developing Spatial Reasoning

Explaining the Concept *(cont.)*

Step 4

Have students discover which regular polygons tessellate.

- Using plain paper, have students cut the papers in half. Have students place a point (dot) in the center of one half of the paper. Have students place a vertex of a regular polygon on the point and trace it as many times as possible by rotating it around the point, with no overlapping. Have students continue tracing the shape until the page is completely covered.

- Have students share with their groups whether or not the shape they chose tessellated. Have them use the table for problem **b** on the activity sheet, *Which Shapes Tessellate?* (page 153), to write whether the shape tessellated.

- Using the other half of the paper, have students choose another regular polygon that has not been used and repeat the steps mentioned above.

- Have each group share findings and record them on the board or overhead.

- Have the groups answer problem **c** on the activity sheet, *Which Shapes Tessellate?* Before reviewing the questions, explain how to calculate if a regular polygon tessellates.

Step 5

Explain how to determine if a regular polygon tessellates.

- Ask students what a vertex angle is. *Answer: A vertex angle is formed by two consecutive sides.*

- Have students write the formula to calculate the degree of a vertex angle. On the activity sheet, *Which Shapes Tessellate? Answer: (n – 2)180/n, where n equals the number of sides of a regular polygon*

- Have students write the number of sides for each polygon on the activity sheet, *Which Shapes Tessellate?* Then have them calculate the vertex angle for each polygon.

- Have students determine if the vertex angle is a divisor of 360 and record *yes* or *no* in the table on the activity sheet, *Which Shapes Tessellate?* Tell students that in order for a regular polygon to form a tessellation, its vertex angle must be a divisor of 360 degrees.

Tessellating with Regular & Irregular Shapes *(cont.)*

Developing Spatial Reasoning

Using the Calculator

Step 1
Have students access the Draw features on the graphing calculator, to create a design that will tessellate.

- Press GRAPH to operate all **Draw** menu features from the Graph screen. **Special Note:** You may need to turn off any previously created Stat Plots or clear any graphs entered in the Y= screen.

- Press 2ND and then PGRM to access **Draw**.

- Press 1 to select **ClrDraw**, which will clear any figures on the Graph screen.

- Return to the Draw menu. Access Draw Pen by scrolling down to **A: Pen**, and pressing ENTER.

Step 2
Explain how to use the Draw Pen feature.

- To turn on the Pen, press ENTER. To turn off the Pen, press ENTER.

- When the Pen is off, the cursor can be moved to any point on the screen without drawing a line. When the Pen is on, a line will be drawn to wherever the cursor is moved.

- To create a horizontal line, use the right and left arrow keys. To create a vertical line use the up and down arrow keys. To create a diagonal line, alternate between pressing the up/down arrows and the left/right arrows.

Step 3
Have students practice using the Draw Pen feature by drawing a triangle.

- Have students draw more triangles around the vertex of the triangle already drawn.

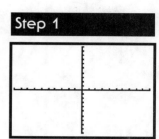

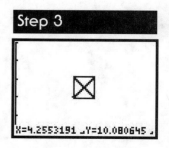

Tessellating with Regular & Irregular Shapes *(cont.)*

Developing Spatial Reasoning

Using the Calculator *(cont.)*

Step 4 Have students create designs on the graphing calculator that will tessellate.

- Have students show their designs to the students in their groups and state two mathematical statements about their tessellations.
- Have students transfer their designs to the dot paper (page 208), and record their mathematical statements at the bottom.

Step 5 Have students complete the activity sheet, *Which Shapes Tessellate?* (page 153).

- Have students compare their predictions to their outcomes.
- Discuss why some shapes tessellate and others do not tessellate.

Applying the Concept

Step 1 Create a list with students of real-life situations using tessellations.

Step 2 Then show students samples of tessellations, such as M.C. Escher's, or pictures of architecture that incorporate tessellations.

Step 3 Have students form groups. Give each group a sample of a tessellation. Have students determine which geometric shape was used to create the tessellation.

- Have the groups share with the class the shape they think Escher used in his tessellation.
- Have students record on chart paper mathematical properties and concepts that they have observed in the pictures of the tessellations.

Step 4 Have students complete the activity sheet, *How to Make a Tessellating Shape* (pages 154–155). Review the problems with the students.

Extension Ideas

- Have students research M.C. Escher and bring in other examples of his work.
- Have students research the art of quilting and investigate the tessellations that exist in quilts as well as the patterns and other mathematical properties and concepts that quilts reflect.

Name _____

Date _____

Which Shapes Tessellate?

Directions: Create a tessellating pattern using the regular polygons. Then follow the steps below to determine which shapes tessellate.

a. Which shape was used in your pattern? _____

_____

b. Use the table below to predict which of the polygons listed might tessellate by writing *yes* or *no* in the second column. Then test which of the polygons tessellate and record *yes* or *no* in the third column.

Shape	Will the polygon tessellate?	Did the polygon tessellate?
Equilateral Triangle		
Quadrilateral (Square)		
Pentagon		
Hexagon		
Octagon		
Decagon		
Dodecagon		

c. Why do you think some shapes tessellate and others do not? _____

_____

d. What is the formula for the vertex angle? _____

e. Complete the table by listing the number of sides and the vertex angles for each shape. Then determine if the vertex angle is a divisor of 360 and record *yes* or *no*.

Shape	Number of Sides	Vertex Angle	Divisor of 360?
Equilateral Triangle			
Quadrilateral (Square)			
Pentagon			
Hexagon			
Octagon			
Decagon			
Dodecagon			

How to Make a Tessellating Shape

Directions: Follow the steps below to create a new shape that tessellates.

Materials

- index card or square piece of cardboard
- scissors
- tape (any type)
- pencil
- construction paper or poster board

Procedure

1. Number the sides 1–4 on the cardboard or the index card.

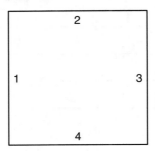

2. Using side 1 of the index card, draw a design from vertex to vertex. Cut out the shape, slide it into place, and tape it to side 3 of the index card.

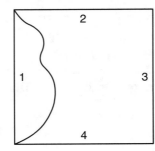 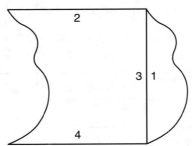

3. Using side 2 of the index card, draw a design from vertex to vertex. Cut out the shape, slide it into place, and tape it to side 4 of the index card.

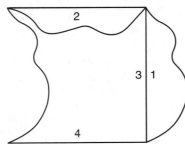 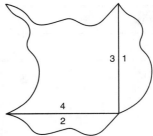

Name

Date

How to Make a Tessellating Shape (cont.)

Procedure (cont.)

4. Determine if you have created a shape that will tessellate. Place the shape on the poster board and trace it. Continue to reposition the shape and trace it until the entire poster board is tessellated.

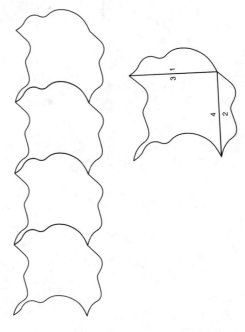

Directions: Answer the questions below about your new shape.

a. Does your shape tessellate? Explain why or why not.

_____

_____

b. Write three mathematical statements about your tessellation, e.g. geometric properties, numbers, algebraic expressions, measurements, etc.

_____

_____

c. What person, place, or thing does your shape look like to you?

_____

Challenge

Try and recreate your shape and/or a portion of your tessellation using the Draw Pen feature on the graphing calculator. Which calculator skills or strategies did you use to recreate your shape or tessellation?

_____

_____

#50026—*Graphing Calculator Strategies, Middle School Math*   © *Shell Education*

Working with Units of Measurement

Working with Units of Measurement

#50026—*Graphing Calculator Strategies, Middle School Math*

Using the Pythagorean Theorem

Working with Units of Measurement

Lesson Description

- Students will understand and use the Pythagorean theorem and its converse to find the length of the missing side of a right triangle.
- Students will use the Pythagorean theorem to find the length of the missing side of a right triangle to calculate the area and perimeter of geometric shapes.

Materials

- *Discover the Pythagorean Theorem* (page 163; msrm163.pdf.)
- *Practice! Practice! Pythagorean Theorem* (page 164; msrm164.pdf)
- *Applying the Pythagorean Theorem* (page 165; msrm165.pdf)
- *Pythagorean Theorem Challenge* (page 166; msrm166.pdf)
- TI-83/84 Plus Family Graphing Calculator or TI-73 Explorer™

Explaining the Concept/Using the Calculator

Step 1

Ask students the following questions:

- What is a right triangle? *Answer: A triangle that has a 90° angle*
- What is the value of 4^2? *Answer: 16*
- What is the square root of 36? *Answer: 6*

Step 2

Students will discover the Pythagorean theorem by using the activity sheet, *Discover the Pythagorean Theorem* (page 163), and a graphing calculator.

- Have students look at the three pictures on the activity sheet.
- Ask the students what type of triangle is shown in each picture. *Answer: Right Triangle*
- Point out to students that squares are formed on each length of the triangle. Ask students how the area of each square can be calculated. *Answer: length times width*
- Ask students what key on the graphing calculator can be used to find the area of a square. Why? *Answer: The* x^2 *key because the length and width are equivalent for a square, and squaring a number is the same as multiplying a number by itself*
- Have all students point to the x^2 on the graphing calculator.

Using the Pythagorean Theorem *(cont.)*

Working with Units of Measurement

Explaining the Concept/Using the Calculator *(cont.)*

Step 3

Have students use the graphing calculator to determine the area of each square for triangle 1 on *Discover the Pythagorean Theorem* (page 163).

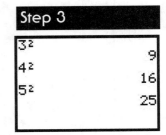

- Explain to students that sides *a* and *b* of the right triangle are called the legs, and side *c* of the right triangle is called the hypotenuse. Therefore, dimensions given for Triangle 1 are

  $a = 3$, $b = 4$, $c = 5$.

- Access the Home screen, by pressing **2ND** and then **MODE** to quit all other screens.

- To calculate the area of the square for *leg a*, press **3** and then **x^2**. Press **ENTER** to execute the expression. Repeat the steps for the squares for *legs b* and *c*.

- The areas for square *a* is 9, for square *b* is 16, and for square *c* is 25. Record these values on the table. Repeat this process for triangles 2 and 3.

Step 4

Using the data gathered in the table on *Discover the Pythagorean Theorem*, have the students answer complete parts.

- After students complete each question, discuss their responses.

Step 5

Using the Pythagorean theorem and the graphing calculator, work problems **f** and **g** from the activity sheet, *Discover the Pythagorean Theorem*.

- In problem **f**, the two legs are given and *c* is the unknown. At this point, ask students whether it matters which leg is labeled *a* or *b*. *Answer: No. Since you are adding the area of the two legs, the order does not matter; a + b = b + a.*

- Have students write in their notes the Pythagorean theorem under problem **f**; then insert the values for *a* and *b*.

$$a^2 + b^2 = c^2$$
$$5^2 + 7^2 = c^2$$

Using the Pythagorean Theorem *(cont.)*

Working with Units of Measurement

Explaining the Concept/Using the Calculator *(cont.)*

Step 6 Have students use the graphing calculator to find the values for 5^2 and 7^2. Then have them add the two products. (Refer to Step 3 for how to use the x^2 key.)

Step 6	
5^2	25
7^2	49
49+25	74
■	

Step 7 Have students calculate the square root of 74 to determine the value of *c*.

- Press **2ND** and then **x^2** to access the square root.

- Type the value for *c*, e.g. **7**, **4**, and then press **ENTER** to evaluate the expression.

- Have students round their answers to the nearest tenth. Ask students, "What does the value 8.6 represent?" *Answer: The length of the hypotenuse for the triangle in* problem f

Step 7	
√(74)	8.602325267
■	

Step 8 Have students write the Pythagorean theorem for problem **g**. Then students should insert the value 10 for *a* and 13 for *c*.

- Explain that in problem **g**, the length of a leg and the hypotenuse are given. Ask students, "Does it matter which variable *a* or *b* is given the value of 10?" *Answer: No.*

$$a^2 + b^2 = c^2$$
$$10^2 + b^2 = 13^2$$

Step 9 Have students calculate 10^2 and 13^2. (Refer to **Step 3** for how to use the x^2 key.)

$$100 + b^2 = 169$$

- Solve for *b* by subtracting 100 from 169.

Step 9	
10^2	100
13^2	169
169-100	69
■	

Using the Pythagorean Theorem *(cont.)*

Working with Units of Measurement

Explaining the Concept/Using the Calculator *(cont.)*

Step 10

Calculate the square root of 69. Round to the nearest tenth. (Refer to **Step 7** for how to calculate a square root.)

$b^2 = 69$ $b = 8.31$

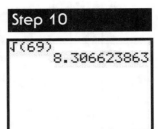

Step 10

√(69)
     8.306623863

Step 11

Have students complete the activity sheet, *Practice! Practice! Pythagorean Theorem* (page 164). Review the problems with the students.

Applying the Concept

Step 1

Have students look around the room for right triangles. Ask students to identify the legs and hypotenuse of the right triangle.

Step 2

Using problem *a* on the activity sheet, *Applying the Pythagorean Theorem* (page 165), model how to use the problem solving skill, drawing a picture, to solve the problem.

- Show students how to extract necessary key words and information for drawing an accurate representation of the problem.

Step 3

Have students complete the activity sheet, *Applying the Pythagorean Theorem*. Review the problems with students.

Step 4

Have students complete the activity sheet, *Pythagorean Theorem Challenge* (page 166). Review the problems with students.

Extension Ideas

- To enhance mental math skills, have students evaluate problems such as perfect squares.

- Have students estimate nonperfect squares. For example: *The answer is going to be between _____ and _____; therefore...*

Discover the Pythagorean Theorem

Directions: In the table below record the type of triangle shown in each picture. Then use the lengths of each triangle to find the area of each square. Record the areas below.

1 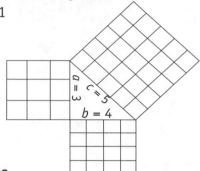 2 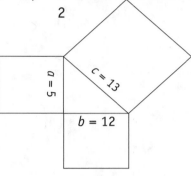 3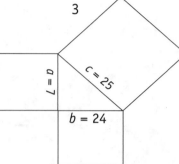

a.

	Triangle	Area of Square for a	Area of Square for b	Area of Square for c
1				
2				
3				

Directions: Using the data gathered, answer the following questions:

b. How are the areas of a and b related to the area of c? _____

c. How was the area of each square calculated? _____

d. Write the length of each square in exponent form in the table below.

Triangle	Area of square a in exponent form	Area of square b in exponent form	Area of square c in exponent form
1			
2			
3			

e. Use the variables a, b, and c to write the Pythagorean theorem.

_____

Directions: Solve using the Pythagorean theorem. Round answers to the nearest tenth.

f.

$a = 5$ cm $c =$ _____

$b = 7$ cm

g.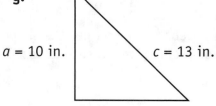

$a = 10$ in. $c = 13$ in.

$b =$ _____

Name _____

Date _____

Practice! Practice! Pythagorean Theorem

Directions: Use the graphing calculator to find the length of the unknown for each triangle. Round the final answer to the nearest tenth.

a.

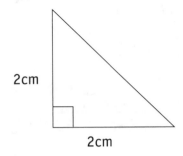

2cm

2cm

b.

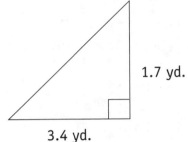

1.7 yd.

3.4 yd.

c.

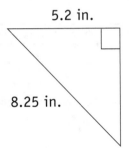

5.2 in.

8.25 in.

d.

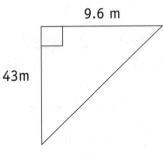

9.6 m

43m

e.

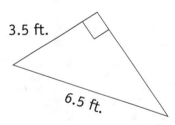

3.5 ft.

6.5 ft.

f.

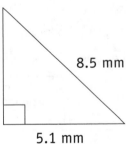

8.5 mm

5.1 mm

Directions: Use the graphing calculator and the Pythagorean theorem to find the unknown side. If necessary, draw a picture.

g. A painter leans the top of a 12-foot ladder against a house. The bottom of the ladder is 5 feet from the house. What is the length from the top of the ladder to the ground?

h. A baseball diamond has the shape of a square. Each side is 90 feet long. What is the length from home plate to second base?

Name _____

Date _____

Applying the Pythagorean Theorem

Directions: Solve the following problems on a separate piece of paper. Round all final answers to the nearest tenth. Draw a picture to help solve the problems.

a. A suitcase measures 23 inches long and 19 inches high. What is the diagonal dimension of the suitcase? Round to the nearest tenth. Explain your answer.

b. Tom wants to buy a new television. He wants to put the television in a cabinet that is 15 inches high and 15 inches wide. Looking through the Sunday ads, he finds a television on sale that he is interested in. The ad states that the screen is 19 inches, which is the diagonal distance across the screen. The height of the screen is 10 inches. What is the width of the screen? Can he purchase this television? Explain why or why not.

c. The hypotenuse of a right triangle is 13 cm and a leg is 5 cm. What is the length of the other leg? Explain your answer.

d. Two joggers run 10 miles north and then 7 miles west. What is the shortest distance they must travel to return to their starting point? Round to the nearest tenth. Justify your answer.

e. Fluffy's doghouse is shaped like a tent. The slanted sides are both 4 feet long and the bottom is 5 feet across. What is the height of the doghouse? Explain your answer.

f. Find the sum of the first 50 odd numbers by first finding the sum of the first odd number (1 = 1), then the sum of the first two odd numbers (1 + 3 = 4), then the sum of the first three odd numbers (1 + 3 + 5 = ?) etc., until you see a pattern. Use the table below to find the pattern.

Number of Odd Numbers	Sum
1	1
2	4
3	
4	
5	
6	
N	
50	

Name _____

Date _____

Pythagorean Theorem Challenge

Directions: Use the graphing calculator and the Pythagorean theorem to find the area and perimeter of each shape. Round all final answers to the nearest tenth.

a.

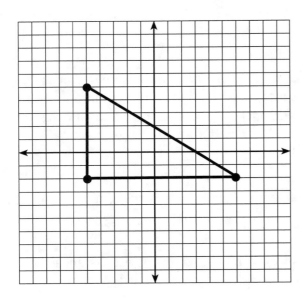

Area = _____

Perimeter = _____

b.

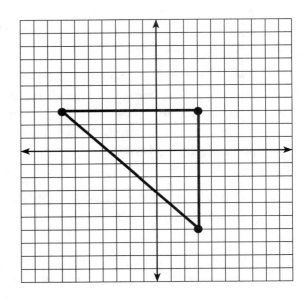

Area = _____

Perimeter = _____

c.

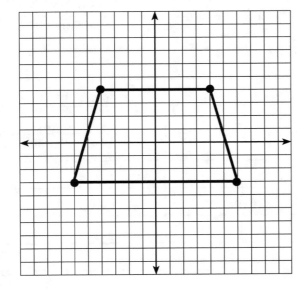

Area = _____

Perimeter = _____

d.

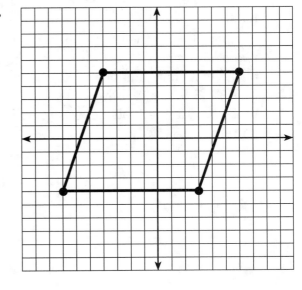

Area = _____

Perimeter = _____

Computing Area and Perimeter

Working with Units of Measurement

Lesson Description

- Students will estimate and compute the area of irregular, two-dimensional shapes by dividing the shapes into regular polygons.

Materials

- *Practice! Practice! Area & Perimeter* (page 170; msrm170.pdf)
- *Irregular Shapes* (page 171; msrm171.pdf)
- *Square Footage* (page 172; msrm172.pdf)
- *Architect's Challenge* (page 173; msrm173.pdf)
- Plain paper (2 pieces)
- Blank overhead (1)
- TI-83/84 Plus Family Graphing Calculator or TI-73 Explorer™

Step 1

Explaining the Concept/Using the Calculator

Ask students the following questions:

- What is area? *Answer: The number of square units needed to cover the surface* How is it denoted? *Answer: in square units*

- What is perimeter? *Answer: The distance around a figure* How is it denoted? *Answer: Units*

Step 2

Use the AreaForm application on the graphing calculator to teach the area of a rectangle, square, parallelogram, triangle, trapezoid, and circle.

- Press **APPS** to access the Applications menu. Scroll down and highlight **AreaForm**. Press **ENTER** to select it.

- Press any key twice to continue. On the Select A Mode screen, press ⌐1⌐ to access **DEFINITIONS & FORMULAS**.

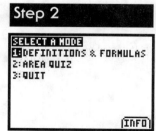

Computing Area and Perimeter *(cont.)*

Working with Units of Measurement

Explaining the Concept/Using the Calculator *(cont.)*

Step 3 Have students practice calculating the area of a rectangle.

- On the Select a Shape screen, press [1] to select **RECTANGLE**. The graphing calculator will give a picture and definition of each shape.

- Press the **AREA** soft key or [WINDOW]. The formula for the area of a rectangle will appear on the screen.

- Have students write the formula for a rectangle on the activity sheet, *Practice! Practice! Area & Perimeter* (page 170).

- Press the **EXAMPLE** soft key or [ZOOM] to view an example of how to calculate the area of a rectangle.

Step 3 *(cont.)*

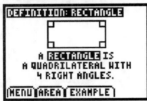

Step 4 Use the example shown on the screen to discuss with students how to calculate the perimeter of the rectangle.

- Explain that to find the perimeter of any polygon they should add the lengths of the sides.

Step 3 *(cont.)*

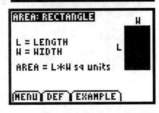

Step 5 For more examples of area, press the **EXAMPLE** soft key or [TRACE] again.

Step 5

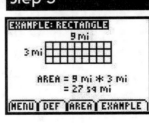

Step 6 Have students repeat **Steps 2–4** to learn how to calculate the areas and perimeter of the other shapes.

- To return to the Select a Shape menu, press the **MENU** soft key.

- Ask students, "Why is the Pythagorean theorem ($a^2 + b^2 = c^2$) used to calculate the perimeter of a parallelogram and trapezoid?"

- Explain to students the formula for the circumference of a circle.

$$C = \pi d \text{ or } C = 2\pi r$$

Step 7 Students should complete the rest of the activity sheet, *Practice! Practice! Area & Perimeter*.

Computing Area and Perimeter *(cont.)*

Working with Units of Measurement

Applying the Concept

Step 1   Using two sheets of plain paper, fold and cut one sheet into two triangles.

Step 2   Holding the two triangles in one hand and the plain sheet of paper in the other, ask students if the area of both the plain piece of paper and the triangles are the same and why or why not. *Answer: Yes, the two triangles when put together are the same size as the plain sheet of paper.*

Step 3   Have a student draw an irregular shape with no curved lines on an overhead. Trace that same irregular shape on a plain piece of paper.

Step 4   Cut the irregular shape drawn on the paper into smaller regular shapes.

- Place the cut-apart regular shapes on top of the overhead of the irregular shape to demonstrate how areas are equivalent.

Step 5   Demonstrate how to calculate the areas of the regular shapes to find the area of the irregular shape.

- Measure the lengths and widths of the regular shapes. Calculate the area of each shape.
- Calculate the sum of the areas to demonstrate how an irregular shape can be broken into smaller parts to find the total area.

Step 6   Model problem **a** on the activity sheet, *Irregular Shapes* (page 171).

- Show how to draw lines to divide an irregular shape into smaller regular shapes.
- Students should complete the remaining problems independently. Have student volunteers model the problems on the overhead.

Step 7   Have students complete *Square Footage* (page 172) with a partner. Review the problems with the students.

Extension Ideas

- Have students complete the activity sheet, *Architect's Challenge* (page 173).
- Measure the area of the walls in the classroom and determine how many gallons of paint are needed to paint all of the walls.
- Measure the perimeter of the classroom and determine how many rolls of decorative border are needed to outline the perimeter of the room.

Name _____

Date _____

Practice! Practice! Area & Perimeter

Directions: Write the area formulas for the listed shapes. Then calculate the area and perimeter of each shape. Hint: To calculate the perimeter, you will need to use the Pythagorean theorem for some of the shapes. Round your final answers to the nearest tenth.

a. What are the area formulas for the following shapes?

Rectangle: _____ Square: _____

Parallelogram: _____ Triangle: _____

Trapezoid: _____ Circle: _____

b.

11.36 cm

17.08 cm

Area = _____

Perimeter = _____

c.

1.7 in.

Area = _____

Perimeter = _____

d.

4 ft.   2 ft.

5 ft.

Area = _____

Perimeter = _____

e.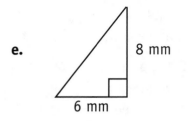

8 mm

6 mm

Area = _____

Perimeter = _____

f.

5 yd

3 yd   7 yd   3 yd

Area = _____

Perimeter = _____

g.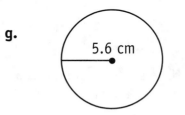

5.6 cm

Area = _____

Circumference = _____

h. Aaron built a square deck that has an area of 240.25 ft². What are the dimensions of the deck? Explain your answer on a separate piece of paper.

i. Kelly wants to build a deck with an area of 255 ft². List all the possible dimensions of the deck. Which dimensions would make the deck functional? Explain your answer on a separate piece of paper.

Name _____

Date _____

Irregular Shapes

Directions: Find the area and perimeter of each irregular shape. When necessary, round answers to the nearest hundredth.

a.

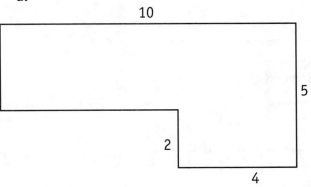

Area = _____

Perimeter = _____

c.

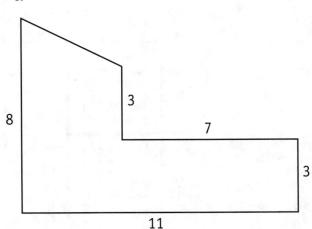

Area = _____

Perimeter = _____

b.

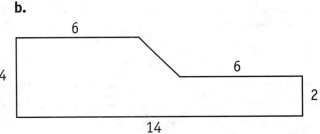

Area = _____

Perimeter = _____

d.

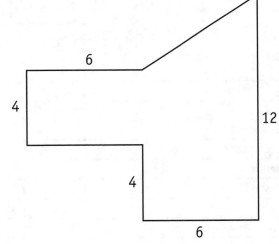

Area = _____

Perimeter = _____

e. Explain the strategies you used to find the area and perimeter of the irregular shapes above.

Name

Date

Square Footage

Directions: Shown below is a floor plan of a home. Use the grid to calculate the area of each room and write it in the table below. Then find the total square footage of the floor plan. Finally, explain how you calculated the areas and the total square footage of the home.

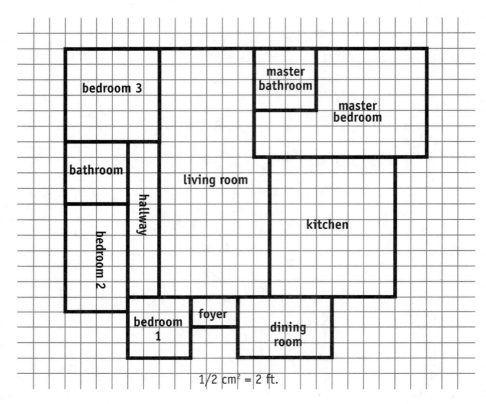

1/2 cm² = 2 ft.

Room	Area	Calculations
Bedroom 1		
Bedroom 2		
Bedroom 3		
Bathroom		
Master Bedroom		
Master Bathroom		
Living Room		
Kitchen		
Dining Room		
Foyer		
Hallway		
Total Area		

On a separate piece of paper explain how you calculated the areas of the rooms and the total area of the floor plan.

#50026—*Graphing Calculator Strategies, Middle School Math*   © *Shell Education*

Name _____

Date _____

Architect's Challenge

Directions: On a separate piece of graph paper, design your own floor plan for a home that you would like to build. Write the scale of your drawing on the graph paper. Record the dimensions of each room and the area in the table below. Then write a description of your home on the lines below.

Use the average room sizes given in the table below to ensure that your dimensions are realistic. The lot for your home site is 12,000 square feet; therefore, the total square footage of your house can be no greater than the square footage of your lot. Remember to leave some space for your yard.

Room	Average size	Your Dimensions	Area
Living Room	19 feet by 8 1/2 feet		
Dining Room	18 feet by 12 feet		
Kitchen	20 feet by 9 feet		
Bedrooms and Bathrooms	500 square feet (total area)		
Other Rooms			
Yard			
Total Square Footage of Home:			

On the lines below, write a description of your home as if you were giving a potential buyer a tour. Include how you determined the scale of the drawing, the dimensions for each room, and the general layout of your home. Explain how you calculated the area of each room and the total area of your home.

_____

_____

_____

_____

_____

_____

_____

_____

Constructing and Reading Scale Drawings

Working with Units of Measurement

Lesson Description
- Students will construct and read scale drawings.
- Students will use a scale to determine the lengths of each side of a geometric shape and then determine the area and perimeter of the shape.

Materials
- **Appendix C**: *Grid paper (1/4 inch)* (page 201; appnd201.pdf)
- *Grid Person* (page 179; msrm179.pdf)
- *Practice! Practice! Scale Drawings* (pages 180–181; msrm180.pdf)
- *Half and Double* (page 182; msrm182.pdf)
- *Classroom Map* (page 183; msrm183.pdf)
- TI-83/84 Plus Family Graphing Calculator or TI-73 Explorer™

Explaining the Concept

Step 1

Ask students the following question:
- What is a scale drawing? *Answer: It is a drawing that shows an object as a ratio of its actual size.*

Step 2

Place a transparency of *Grid Person* (page 179) on the overhead or give each student a copy. Give each student a piece of graph paper.
- On a separate piece of graph paper, have half of the students double the length and width of each rectangle and square on *Grid Person*.
- On another sheet of graph paper, have the other half of the students add 2 units to the length and width of each rectangle and square on Grid Person.

Step 3

Once the students have completed their new *Grid Person*, place the ones that were doubled on one side of the classroom and place the others on the other side of the classroom.
- Ask students which Grid Person looks the same as the original, but larger. *Answer: The Grid Person that was doubled*
- Ask students, "How would you change the *Grid Person* that was doubled to look like the original?" *Answer: Take half of the length and the width of each rectangle and square*
- Ask students, "Why does doubling, or taking half of the rectangle or square on *Grid Person*, look the same as the original, but not adding or subtracting two from each rectangle or square?" *Answer: Doubling, or taking half, is proportional to the original dimensions of Grid Person. Adding or subtracting two is not increasing all the dimensions by the same proportion.*

Constructing and Reading Scale Drawings (cont.)

Working with Units of Measurement

Explaining the Concept (cont.)

Step 4

Use *Grid Person* to model how to write a portion to calculate the dimensions for a drawing with a scale 1:2.

- Determine the length of each side on the original Grid Person and the double Grid Person.

$$\frac{1}{2} = \frac{16}{x} \qquad x = 32$$

Step 5

If one unit on the original Grid Person equals 3.5 centimeters, then what is the length of each side of Grid Person?

$$\frac{1}{3.5} = \frac{16}{x} \qquad x = 56$$

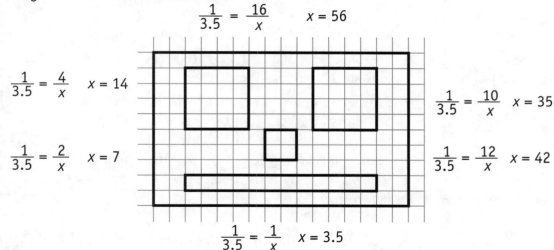

$$\frac{1}{3.5} = \frac{4}{x} \quad x = 14$$

$$\frac{1}{3.5} = \frac{2}{x} \quad x = 7$$

$$\frac{1}{3.5} = \frac{10}{x} \quad x = 35$$

$$\frac{1}{3.5} = \frac{12}{x} \quad x = 42$$

$$\frac{1}{3.5} = \frac{1}{x} \quad x = 3.5$$

Step 6

On a piece of graph paper, have students draw a rectangle that is 4 x 8 units.

- Have students double the dimensions of the rectangle. *Answer: 8 x 16 units*
- Have a student draw the new rectangle and its dimensions on the board.
- Ask students, "What is the area and perimeter of the new rectangle?" *Answer: 128 units² and 48 units*
- Have students decrease the dimensions of the original rectangle by half. *Answer: 2 x 4 units*
- Have a student draw the new rectangle with its dimensions on the board.
- Ask students, "What is the area and the perimeter of the new rectangle?" *Answer: 8 units² and 12 units*
- Have students calculate the length and width of the 4 x 8 units rectangle using the scale of 1:2.5. *Answer: 10 x 20 units*
- Ask students, "What is the area and the perimeter of the new rectangle?" *Answer: 200 units² and 60 units*

Constructing and Reading Scale Drawings *(cont.)*

Working with Units of Measurement

Using the Calculator

Step 1

Using problem **a** on *Practice! Practice! Scale Drawings*, and a graphing calculator, model each step of the problem with the students.

- Access the Stat List editor by pressing **STAT** and then ⓵ .

- Input the ordered pairs into the Stat List editor by typing the number and pressing **ENTER**. Use **L1** for the *x*-coordinates and **L2** for the *y*-coordinates.

Step 2

Set up a line graph in the Stat Plot editor.

- Press the **2ND** and then **Y=** to access the Stat Plot editor. Choose **Plot1**.

- Select the following settings by highlighting each and pressing **ENTER**. Turn **On** the plot. By **Type**, select the line graph, which is the second icon. By **Xlist**, input **L1** (**2ND** , ⓵). By **Ylist**, input **L2** (**2ND** , ⓶). By **Mark**, select the first icon (square).

Step 3

Have students view and analyze the graph in an appropriate window.

- Press **ZOOM** and then ⑥ to view this graph in a **ZStandard** window.

- Ask the students what shape was created. *Answer: square*

Step 4

Have students double each side of the square. Ask students what strategy they could use to determine the coordinate pairs for the new figure.

- Students should write the new ordered pairs in the **Shape B** table on the *Practice! Practice! Scale Drawings* (pages 180–181).

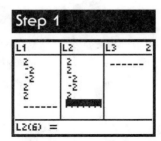

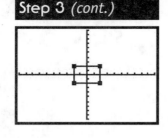

Constructing and Reading Scale Drawings *(cont.)*

Working with Units of Measurement

Using the Calculator *(cont.)*

Step 5

Have students create the doubled square on the graphing calculator.

- Input the coordinates into the graphing calculator Use **L3** for the *x*-coordinates and **L4** for the *y*-coordinates.

- Access the Stat Plot editor and turn on **Plot2** to create the figure. Select the line graph icon. By **Xlist**, input **L3** (**2ND**, **3**) and input **L4** (**2ND**, **4**) by **Ylist**.

Step 6

Have students view and analyze the graph of both figures.

- Press **GRAPH** to view the figure.

- Ask students what the ratio of the larger figure is to the smaller figure. *Answer: 2:1*.

- Ask students how they know that both dimensions (length and width) are the same proportion.

Step 7

Have students use the steps above to complete problems **d–k** on *Practice! Practice! Scale Drawings* (pages 180–181).

Step 8

Have students complete the activity sheet *Half and Double* (page 182).

- Have small groups present the shapes they created on the calculator with the coordinate points on chart paper.

- Groups should share other mathematical statements that they can make about the shapes, coordinates, or shortcuts on the graphing calculator.

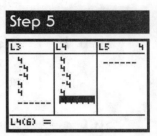

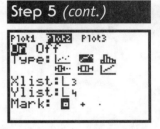

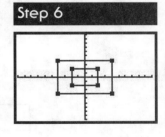

Constructing and Reading Scale Drawings *(cont.)*

Working with Units of Measurement

Applying the Concept

Step 1   Ask students why making a table would be a good problem-solving strategy. *Answer: Responses may vary. A possible answer may include: It helps to organize information and retrieve necessary information quickly and easily.*

Step 2   Explain to students when creating a table that information must be organized into categories that form the columns and rows of the table.

Step 3   Read the activity sheet, *Classroom Map* (page 183).

- Ask students, "What general information or categories of information will we need to complete this activity?"

Step 4   In small groups, have students create a table to organize the information that they will need to create a scale drawing of their classroom and teacher's desk. (Refer to the table below as an example.)

- Have each group draw their table on the activity sheet, *Classroom Map,* and present their table to the class when they are finished.

	Actual Measurement		Scale Measurement	
	Length	**Width**	**Length**	**Width**
Classroom				
Teacher's Desk				

Step 5   Have students work in groups to complete the activity sheet, *Classroom Map.* Have students present their scale drawings to the class.

Extension Ideas

- Have students transfer the table they created on *Classroom Map* to the graphing calculator using the CelSheet application or the Stat List editor.
- Have students make a scale drawing of their bedrooms.

Name _____

Date _____

Grid Person

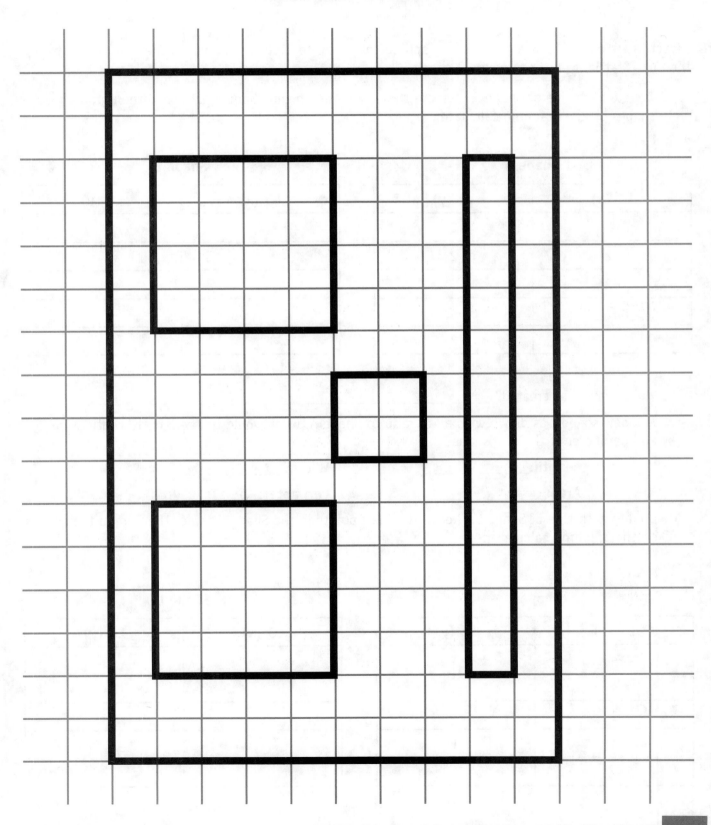

Practice! Practice! Scale Drawings

Directions: For problems a–c, use the graphing calculator to input the points in the Stat List editor then use Stat Plot editor to create a shape.

a. Double each side of Shape A. Record the new points in the Shape B table and then graph both shapes on the graphing calculator.

<table>
<tr><td colspan="2" align="center">**Shape A**</td><td colspan="2" align="center">**Shape B**</td></tr>
<tr><td>**L1 (x)**</td><td>**L2 (y)**</td><td>**L3 (x)**</td><td>**L4 (y)**</td></tr>
<tr><td>2</td><td>2</td><td></td><td></td></tr>
<tr><td>–2</td><td>2</td><td></td><td></td></tr>
<tr><td>–2</td><td>–2</td><td></td><td></td></tr>
<tr><td>2</td><td>–2</td><td></td><td></td></tr>
<tr><td>2</td><td>2</td><td></td><td></td></tr>
</table>

b. What shape was created? _____

c. If a new shape was drawn with a 1:3 ratio to Shape A, what would be the length, width, area, and perimeter of the new shape?

  Length: _____   **Width:** _____

  Area: _____   **Perimeter:** _____

d. Double each side of Shape C. Record the new points in the Shape D table. Then graph the shapes on the graphing calculator.

<table>
<tr><td colspan="2" align="center">**Shape C**</td><td colspan="2" align="center">**Shape D**</td></tr>
<tr><td>**L1 (x)**</td><td>**L2 (y)**</td><td>**L3 (x)**</td><td>**L4 (y)**</td></tr>
<tr><td>–4</td><td>1</td><td></td><td></td></tr>
<tr><td>–4</td><td>–3</td><td></td><td></td></tr>
<tr><td>1</td><td>–3</td><td></td><td></td></tr>
<tr><td>1</td><td>1</td><td></td><td></td></tr>
<tr><td>–4</td><td>1</td><td></td><td></td></tr>
</table>

Name _____

Date _____

Practice! Practice! Scale Drawings *(cont.)*

e. What shape is created? _____

f. If a new shape was drawn with a 2:5.5 ratio to shape C, what would be the length, width, area and perimeter of the new shape?

Length:_____   **Width:** _____

Area:_____   **Perimeter:** _____

g. Calculate half of each side of Shape E. Record the new points in the table for Shape F and then graph both shapes on the graphing calculator.

Shape E

L1 (*x*)	L2 (*y*)
−8	6
−8	−6
8	−6
8	6
−8	6

Shape F

L3 (*x*)	L4 (*y*)

h. What shape is created? _____

i. If a new shape was drawn with a 1:0.25 ratio to Shape E, what would be the length, width, area, and perimeter of the new shape?

Length:_____   **Width:** _____

Area:_____   **Perimeter:** _____

j. Explain the strategy you used to determine the new coordinates for each of the shapes above.

_____

_____

_____

k. Explain the strategy you used to calculate the length, width, area, and perimeter of the shapes that you created.

_____

_____

_____

Name _____

Date _____

Half and Double

Directions: For problems a, b, and c use the graphing calculator to input the points in the Stat List editor. Then, use Stat Plot editor to create a shape.

   a. Create a right triangle in the 3rd quadrant. Record the points in Table 1.

   b. Double the triangle in the 1st quadrant. Record the points in Table 2.

   c. Take half of the triangle in the 4th quadrant. Record the points in Table 3.

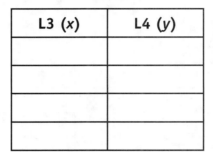

Table 1	
L1 (x)	**L2 (y)**

Table 2	
L3 (x)	**L4 (y)**

Table 3	
L5 (x)	**L6 (y)**

   d. If the ratio is 2:5 for the right triangle created in Table 1, what are the area and perimeter for the shape?

        Area: _____   **Perimeter:** _____

   e. Create a trapezoid in the 2nd quadrant. Record the points in Table 4.

   f. Double the trapezoid in the 3rd quadrant. Record the points in Table 5.

   g. Halve the trapezoid in the 1st quadrant. Record the points in Table 6.

Table 4	
L1 (x)	**L2 (y)**

Table 5	
L3 (x)	**L4 (y)**

Table 6	
L5 (x)	**L6 (y)**

   h. If the ratio is 1:3 for the trapezoid created in Table 4, what are the area and perimeter for the shape?

        Area: _____   **Perimeter:** _____

Name _____

Date _____

Classroom Map

Directions: Create a table in the box below to organize the information needed to create a classroom map. To create the map, plot the points on the coordinate plane and input them into the graphing calculator.

a. Measure the length and width of your classroom. Write the measurements in the table.

b. Determine the scale for the classroom to fit on the coordinate grid above. Draw the length and width. Label the corners as ordered pairs. Input these points into your graphing calculator to create the classroom.

c. Measure the length and width of the teacher's desk. Record the measurements in the table.

d. Determine the scale for the teacher's desk. Draw the length and width. Label the corners as ordered pairs. Input these points into your graphing calculator to create the teacher's desk.

e. Use points on the coordinate plane to represent the students' desks. Draw the points and label each ordered pair. Then input them into the graphing calculator.

f. Write three additional mathematical statements about your classroom map below.

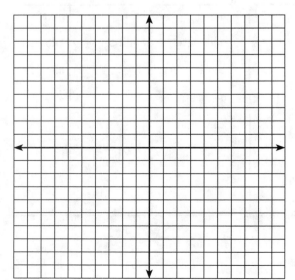

_____

_____

_____

_____

_____

_____

_____

Developing a Sense of Customary & Metric Units

Working with Units of Measurement

Lesson Description

- Students will compare and convert length, weights, and capacities, within and between customary and metric measurement systems.
- Students will discover benchmarks and develop estimation strategies for customary and metric units of measurement.

Materials

- Ruler (one per student)
- Various items to weigh (same items per group)
- *Benchmarks for Customary & Metric Units* (pages 190–191; msrm190.pdf)
- *Practice! Practice! Customary & Metric Units* (pages 192; msrm192.pdf)
- *Scavenger Hunt* (page 193; msrm193.pdf)
- TI-83/84 Plus Family Graphing Calculator or TI-73 Explorer™

Explaining the Concept/Using the Calculator

Step 1

Ask students the following questions:

- How are length, capacity, and weight measured in customary and metric units? Write the units on the board or overhead.

Customary Units

Length	Capacity	Weight
inch	teaspoon	ounce
foot	tablespoon	pound
yard	fluid once	ton
mile	cup	
	pint	
	quart	
	half gallon	
	gallon	

Metric Units

Length	Capacity	Mass
meter	liter	gram
millimeter	milliliter	kilogram
centimeter		metric ton
decimeter		
kilometer		

Developing a Sense of Customary & Metric Units *(cont.)*

Working with Units of Measurement

Explaining the Concept/Using the Calculator *(cont.)*

Step 2   Have students estimate the length of a string and then compare their estimates to the actual length of the string.

- Hold up a piece of string that is 6 inches long. Ask students to estimate the length of the string in inches and centimeters.

- Have them write their estimated lengths on the activity sheet, *Benchmarks for Customary & Metric Units* (pages 190–191).

- Have a student volunteer measure the string in inches. Have students write the actual measurement on the *Benchmarks for Customary & Metric Units*. Ask students how many estimated close to 6 inches.

- Give each group a ruler.

Step 3   Have students work in groups of 3 or 4 to determine how many centimeters are in 6 inches.

- Have each group share their findings.

Step 4   Have students use SciTools in the Applications menu on the graphing calculator to determine how many centimeters are in 6 inches.

- Press the **APPS** key. Scroll down and select the **SciTools**.

- After pressing any key to continue, press ⌐2⌐ to select the **UNIT CONVERTER**.

- On the Unit Converter menu, press ⌐1⌐ to select **length**.

Special Note: To quit a screen and go back, press **2ND** *and then* **MODE** *.*

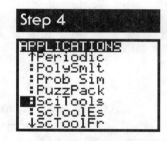

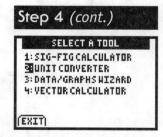

Lesson 20

Developing a Sense of Customary & Metric Units *(cont.)*

Working with Units of Measurement

Explaining the Concept/Using the Calculator *(cont.)*

Step 5

Have students convert 6 inches into centimeters.

- Press **6** to input the number of units. Highlight **in** and then press **ENTER** to select the units that are being converted from.

- Highlight **cm** and then press **ENTER** to select the units to which they are being converted.

- Explain to students that **E1** indicates they need to move the decimal one place to the right to get the answer of *15.24 cm*.

> **Step 5**
>
> | LENGTH | | | | |
> |---|---|---|---|---|
> | fm | Å | mm | **cm** | m |
> | km | Mil | in | ft | yd |
> | fath | rd | mi | nmi | ltyr |
>
> GEO in►
>   1.524E1 cm
>
> CONSTANT EXPT COPY EDIT

Step 6

Have students discover benchmarks for lengths in customary and metric units.

- In small groups, students should work together to find 3 benchmarks.

- As a class, discuss any strategies students may use to estimate length.

- Have students measure body parts, such as length of thumb to pinky finger, length of foot, length of finger, or length of arm span, to discover benchmarks for customary and metric lengths.

- Have students record these benchmarks along with the approximate customary lengths and metric lengths of each on the activity sheet, *Benchmarks for Customary & Metric Units* (pages 190–191).

Step 7

Have students estimate capacities of containers in customary and metric units and compare their estimations to the actual capacities.

- Display four empty containers, such as gallon, liter, pint, or cup. Write the capacity of each container on a piece of paper then tape it to the container so it is not visible to students. Label four of the containers A, B, C, and D.

- Have students write their estimated capacities on the activity sheet, *Benchmarks for Customary & Metric Units*. Discuss their estimations and any strategies they used.

- Ask a student volunteer to share the actual capacities of the containers. Have students write the capacities on the *Benchmarks for Customary & Metric Units* activity sheet.

#50026—Graphing Calculator Strategies, Middle School Math   © *Shell Education*

Developing a Sense of Customary & Metric Units *(cont.)*

Working with Units of Measurement

Explaining the Concept/Using the Calculator *(cont.)*

Step 8

In groups, have students determine two benchmarks or strategies they can use to estimate capacity for customary and metric units.

- Have students place these benchmarks along with the approximate customary capacity and metric capacity of each, on the activity sheet *Benchmarks for Customary & Metric Units* (pages 190–191).

Step 9

Have students use the Unit Converter in the SciTools application on the graphing calculator to convert capacities of customary and metric units of measurement.

- Refer to **Step 4** for instructions on accessing and using the Unit Converter.

- Convert 1 gallon to liters. On the **UNIT CONVERTER** menu, press `3` to select **VOLUME**.

- Press `1` for the number of units. Select **gal** for the units from which they are being converted. Select **L** for the units to which they are being converted.

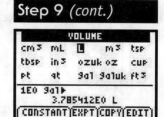

Step 10

Have students work in small groups to estimate the weights of a variety of items in customary and metric units and compare their estimations to the actual weights.

- The items should be the same for each group.

- Students should record the estimations on the *Benchmarks for Customary & Metric Units* activity sheet.

- Have students use a scale to find the actual mass of each item. Students should write the masses on the activity sheet, *Benchmarks for Customary & Metric Units*.

Step 11

In groups, have students determine two benchmarks to estimate mass for customary and metric units.

- Have students write these benchmarks along with the approximate customary mass and metric mass of each on *Benchmarks for Customary & Metric Units*.

Developing a Sense of Customary & Metric Units *(cont.)*

Working with Units of Measurement

Explaining the Concept/Using the Calculator *(cont.)*

Step 12

Have students use the Unit Converter on the graphing calculator to convert mass and weight of customary and metric units of measurement.

- Refer to **Step 4** for instructions on accessing and using the Unit Converter.

- Convert 50 pounds (lbs) to kilograms (kg).

- Press ⌷ 7 ⌷ to select **MASS**.

- Press ⌷ 5 ⌷ ⌷ 0 ⌷ for the number of units.

- Select **lbm** and then select **kg**.

- Remind students to move the decimal one place to the right for the answer.

Step 13

Have students complete the activity sheet, *Practice! Practice! Customary & Metric Units* (page 192). Review the problems with the students.

Applying the Concept

Step 1

Bring in a variety of items still in the original packaging, such as boxed and canned food (measured in net weight), toilet paper or paper towels (measured in length), and any bottled liquid (measured in volume/capacity).

- Display the items for students to see, but cover the measurements.

Step 2

Have the students make a list of the items on paper.

- Ask the students to list the unit of measurement that they think is on the package, either length, weight, or capacity, for both customary and metric units.

- Compare students' answers with what is given on the packaging. Discuss why the units are used for the different products.

Developing a Sense of Customary & Metric Units *(cont.)*

Working with Units of Measurement

Step 3

Applying the Concept *(cont.)*

Students should complete the activity sheet, *Scavenger Hunt* (page 193).

- Prior to the activity, measure two classroom items for the following units of measurement: metric and customary length, metric mass, customary weight, metric and customary capacity.

- Record the items with their measurements on a separate piece of paper as an answer key. List the table name and the corresponding measurements on the board. Do not list the name of the item.

- Have students record the measurements in the tables on the activity sheet.

Extension Idea

To develop students' estimation skills and sense of metric units, set up the following estimation centers:

- Weight Station: Have students guess the weight of various items in grams and pounds.

- How Many? Station: Have students estimate the number of beans, marbles, etc., in a clear jar. Students should record their estimates on a stem-and-leaf plot.

- Length Station: Have students estimate the length of various items in inches and centimeters.

- Volume Station: Have students use a few centimeter cubes to estimate the volume of rectangular prisms.

- History of Measurement Station: Have students research how people measured items before the customary and metrics units were developed.

Benchmarks for Customary & Metric Units

Directions: In the first table estimate the length, capacity, and mass weight of objects and then record the actual number of units. In the second table list benchmarks in customary and metric units that can be used for estimating.

a. Length

	Customary	**Metric**
Estimated Length		
Actual Length		

Benchmark	**Customary**	**Metric**

b. Capacity

	A	**B**	**C**	**D**
Estimated Capacity— Customary				
Actual Capacity— Customary				
Estimated Capacity— Metric				
Actual Capacity— Metric				

Name _____

Date _____

Benchmarks for Customary & Metric Units (cont.)

b. Capacity (cont.)

Benchmark	Customary	Metric

c. Mass

	A	B	C	D
Estimated Mass—Customary				
Actual Mass—Customary				
Estimated Mass—Metric				
Actual Mass—Metric				

Benchmark	Customary	Metric

Name _____

Date _____

Practice! Practice! Customary & Metric Units

Directions: Use the Unit Converter in the SciTools applications on the graphing calculator. Solve the following problems.

a. 3 feet = _____ inches = _____ centimeters

b. 6 meters = _____ centimeters = _____ feet

c. 4 gallons = _____ pints = _____ liters

d. 1637 milliliters = _____ liters = _____ pints

e. 413 kilograms = _____ grams = _____ pounds

f. 3468 grams = _____ kilograms = _____ pounds

Directions: Use the height-weight information about Shaquille O'Neal and Venus Williams to answer the questions below.

Shaquille O'Neal is a basketball player in the NBA. He weighs 325 pounds and is 7'1". Venus Williams is a professional tennis player. She weighs 72.6 kilograms and is 1.8 meters tall.

g. What is Shaquille's weight in kilograms?

_____

h. What is Venus's weight in pounds?

_____

i. What is Shaquille's weight in grams? Venus's?

_____

j. What is Shaquille's height in meters?

_____

k. What is Venus's height in feet?

_____

l. What is Shaquille's height in inches? Venus's?

_____

m. What is Shaquille's height in centimeters? Venus's?

_____

n. How much more does Shaquille weigh than Venus, in pounds and kilograms?

_____

o. How much taller is Shaquille than Venus, in inches and centimeters.

_____

#50026—Graphing Calculator Strategies, Middle School Math © *Shell Education*

Scavenger Hunt

Directions: The teacher will help you complete the first column of each table. He or she will give you a measurement and you will have to look around the room for an item that is close to the given measurement. Once you have the items listed, go and find the actual length, capacity, or mass and then calculate the difference.

a.

Metric Length	Item	Actual Metric Length	Difference

b.

Customary Length	Item	Actual Customary Length	Difference

c.

Metric Mass	Item	Actual Metric Mass	Difference

d.

Customary Weight	Item	Actual Customary Weight	Difference

e.

Metric Capacity	Item	Actual Metric Capacity	Difference

f.

Customary Capacity	Item	Actual Customary Capacity	Difference

#50026—*Graphing Calculator Strategies, Middle School Math*

Appendices

Florian, J.E., and C.B. Dean. 2001. *Standards in Classroom Practice Research Synthesis: Chapter 2, Mathematics Standards in Classroom Practice*. McREL Publishing.

National Council of Teachers of Mathematics. 2000. *Principles and Standards for School Mathematics: Number and Operations Standard*.

National Council of Mathematics Teachers. 2003. *NCTM Position Statement: The Use of Technology in the Learning and Teaching of Mathematics*. October.

National Council of Mathematics Teachers. 2005. *NCTM Position Statement: Highly Qualified Teachers*. July.

Marzano, R. J. 2003. *What Works in Schools: Translating Research into Action*. Alexandria, VA: Association for Supervision and Curriculum Development.

Seely, C. 2004. *Engagement as a Tool for Equity. NCTM News Bulletin*. Reston, VA: National Council of Teachers of Mathematics. November.

Sutton, J. and A. Krueger. 2002. *EDThoughts: What We Know About Mathematics Teaching and Learning*. Aurora, CO: Mid-continent Research for Education and Learning.

Waits, B. and F. Demana. 1998. *The Role of Graphing Calculators in Mathematics Reform*. Colombus, OH: The Ohio State University. (ERIC Document Reproduction Service No. ED458108).

Waits, B. and H. Pomerantz. 1997. *The Role of Calculators in Math Education*. Colombus, OH: The Ohio State University. Prepared for the Urban Systemic Initiative/ Comprehensive partnership for Mathematics and Science Achievement (USI/CPMSA). Retrieved September 12, 2006 from *http://education.ti.com/educationportal/sites/US/nonProductSingle/ research_therole.html*

Teacher Resource CD Index

Activity Sheet Title	Filename	Activity Sheet Title	Filename
Lesson 1		**Lesson 8**	
Practice! Practice! Order of Operations	nmbrs35.pdf	Practice! Practice! Intersecting Lines	algbr91.pdf
Order of Operations Challenge	nmbrs36.pdf	Applying Intersecting Lines	algbr92.pdf
Cross-Number Puzzle	nmbrs37.pdf	**Lesson 9**	
Lesson 2		Practice! Practice! Stem-and-Leaf Plot	data99.pdf
Practice! Practice! Percents	nmbrs42.pdf	Ballpark Capacity	data100.pdf
Fractions, Decimals, & Percents	nmbrs43.pdf	What Is in Your Cereal Box?	data101.pdf
Final Grade	nmbrs44.pdf	**Lesson 10**	
Grade Sheet	nmbrs45.pdf	Practice! Practice! Probability	data107.pdf
Lesson 3		Fair or Not?	data108.pdf
Practice! Practice! Ratios & Proportions	nmbrs49.pdf	SPIN-O Game	data110.pdf
Jambalaya Proportions	nmbrs50.pdf	**Lesson 11**	
Applying Ratios & Proportions	nmbrs52.pdf	Practice! Practice! Box-and-Whisker Plot	data114.pdf
How Many Fish? Hands on Activity	nmbrs53.pdf	NFL Games	data115.pdf
Lesson 4		More Box-and-Whisker Plots	data117.pdf
Practice! Practice! Integers	nmbrs60.pdf	**Lesson 12**	
More Integers	nmbrs61.pdf	Practice! Practice! Circle Graphs	data123.pdf
Cover Up Numbers Game	nmbrs63.pdf	Survey Says	data125.pdf
Lesson 5		How Do You Spend Your Day?	data126.pdf
Patterns and Equations	algbr71.pdf	**Lesson 13**	
Practice! Practice! Equations of a Line	algbr72.pdf	Practice! Practice! Coordinate Planes	sptl132.pdf
Walking the Line	algbr73.pdf	Plotting Points	sptl133.pdf
Lesson 6		How Many Shapes?	sptl134.pdf
Practice! Practice! Lines	algbr77.pdf	**Lesson 14**	
Where Do We Meet?	algbr78.pdf	Practice! Practice! Transformations	sptl139.pdf
Which Graph?	algbr79.pdf	Transforming Shapes	sptl140.pdf
Lesson 7		Rotations Game	sptl141.pdf
Practice! Practice! Expressions	algbr84.pdf	**Lesson 15**	
Applying Expressions	algbr85.pdf	Practice! Practice! Volume	sptl145.pdf
Investing It	algbr86.pdf	Voluminous Boxes	sptl147.pdf
		Colored Cubes	sptl148.pdf

Activity Sheet Title	Filename
Lesson 16	
Which Shapes Tessellate?	sptl153.pdf
How to Make a Tessellating Shape?	sptl154.pdf
Lesson 17	
Discover the Pythagorean Theorem	msrm163.pdf
Practice! Practice! Pythagorean Theorem	msrm164.pdf
Applying the Pythagorean Theorem	msrm165.pdf
Pythagorean Theorem Challenge	msrm166.pdf
Lesson 18	
Practice! Practice! Area & Perimeter	msrm170.pdf
Irregular Shapes	msrm171.pdf
Square Footage	msrm172.pdf
Architect's Challenge	msrm173.pdf
Lesson 19	
Grid Person	msrm179.pdf
Practice! Practice! Scale Drawings	msrm180.pdf
Half and Double	msrm182.pdf
Classroom Map	msrm183.pdf
Lesson 20	
Benchmarks for Customary & Metric Units	msrm190.pdf
Practice! Practice! Customary & Metric Units	msrm192.pdf
Scavenger Hunt	msrm193.pdf

Appendices	Filename
Decimal Squares	appnd199.pdf
Chips	appnd200.pdf
Grid Paper (1/4 Inch)	appnd201.pdf
Centimeter Grid Paper (1 Centimeter)	appnd202.pdf
Large Coordinate Plane	appnd203.pdf
Small Coordinate Planes	appnd204.pdf
Pattern Blocks	appnd205.pdf
Cube Pattern	appnd206.pdf
Regular Polygons	appnd207.pdf
Dot Paper	appnd208.pdf
Inch Rulers and Yard Stick	appnd209.pdf
Centimeter Rulers	appnd210.pdf
Glossary	appnd211.pdf

Templates & Manipulatives

Decimal Squares

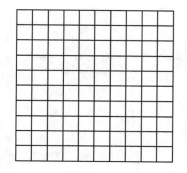 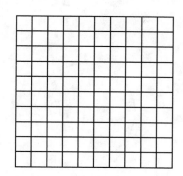 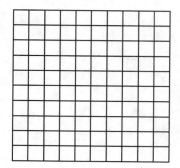

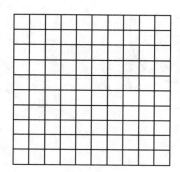 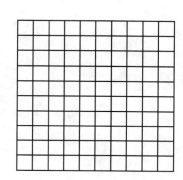 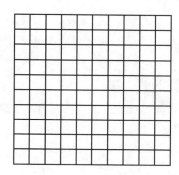

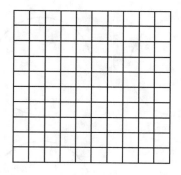 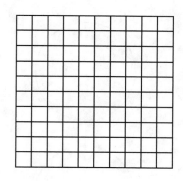 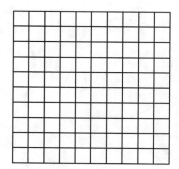

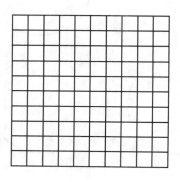 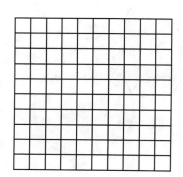 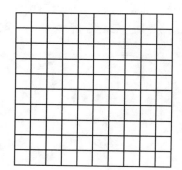

#50026—*Graphing Calculator Strategies, Middle School Math*

Templates & Manipulatives *(cont.)*

Chips

#50026—Graphing Calculator Strategies, Middle School Math

Grid Paper (1/4 Inch)

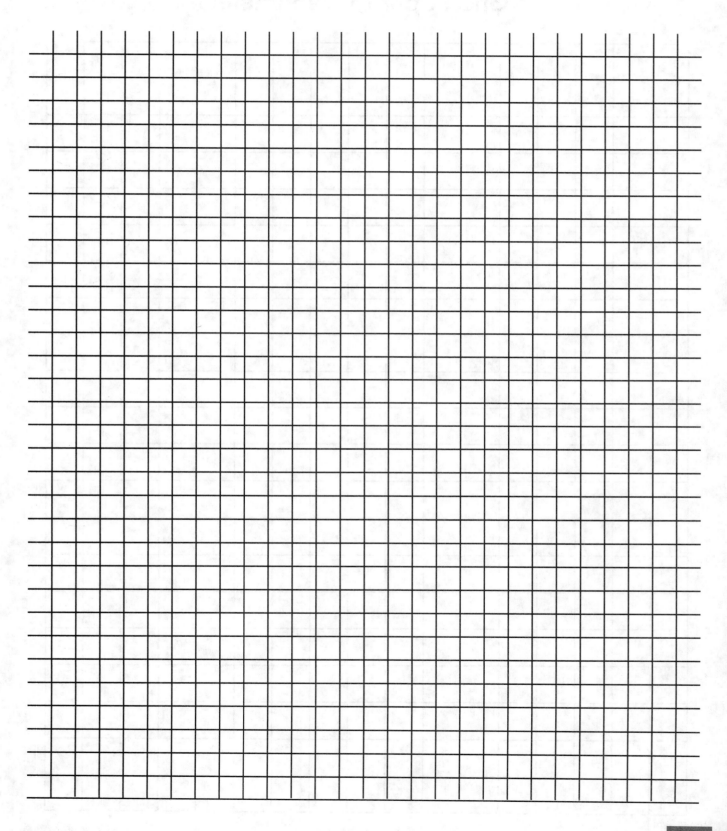

Templates & Manipulatives *(cont.)*

Grid Paper (1 Centimeter)

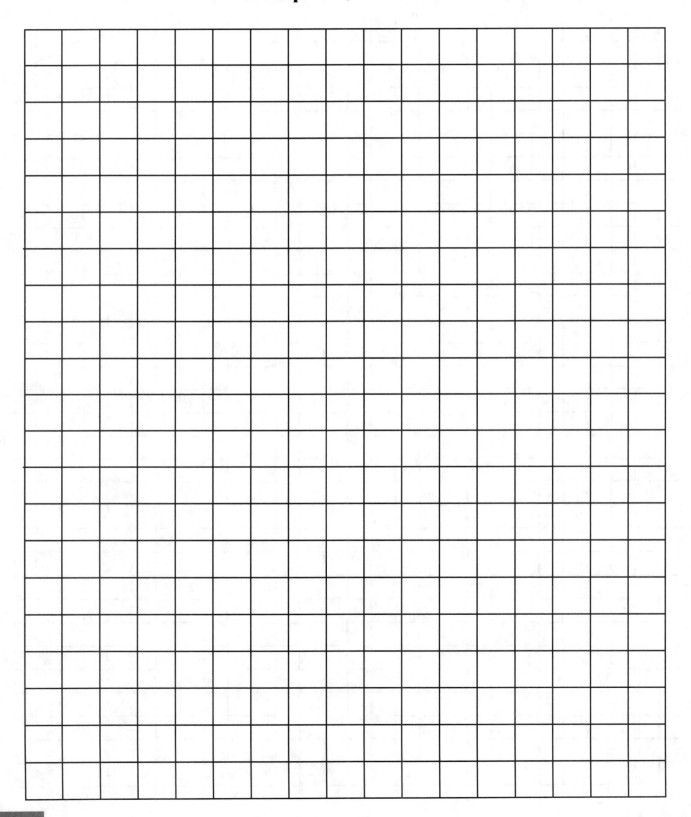

#50026—Graphing Calculator Strategies, Middle School Math

Templates & Manipulatives *(cont.)*

Large Coordinate Plane

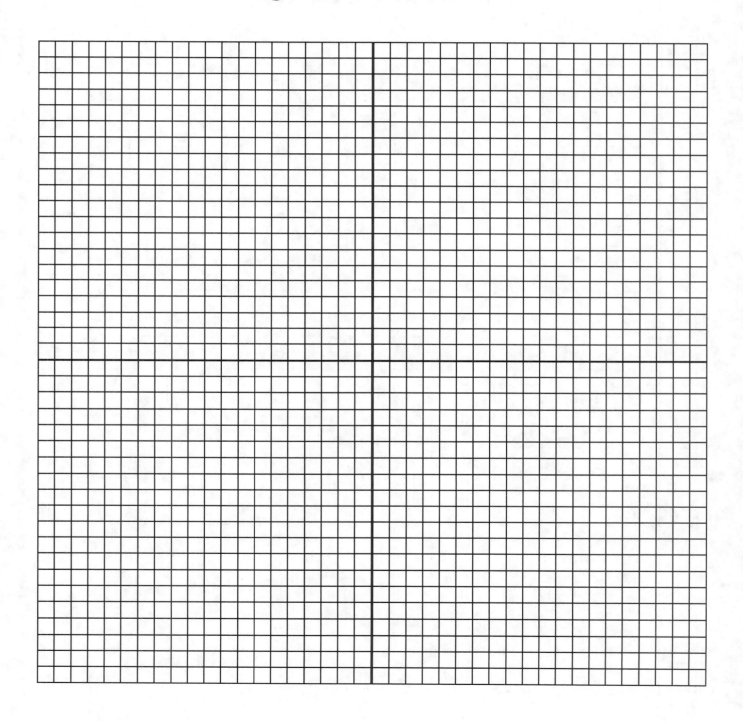

Templates & Manipulatives *(cont.)*

Small Coordinate Planes

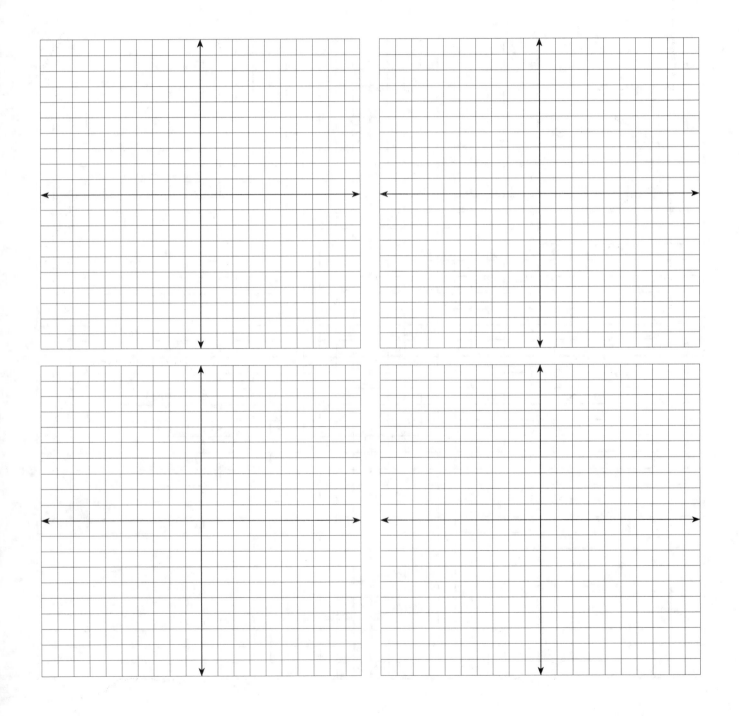

#50026—*Graphing Calculator Strategies, Middle School Math* © *Shell Education*

Pattern Blocks

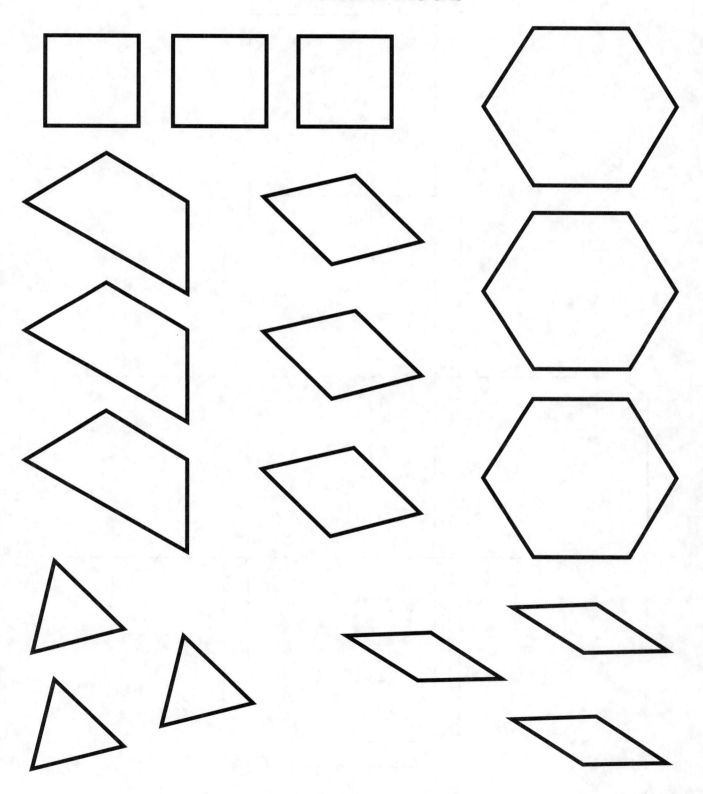

Templates & Manipulatives *(cont.)*

Cube Pattern

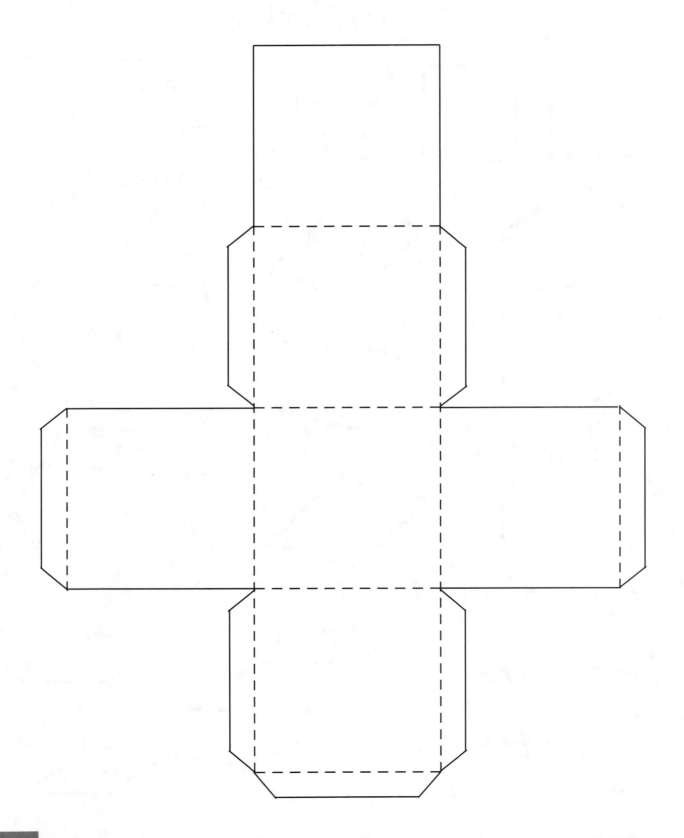

#50026—*Graphing Calculator Strategies, Middle School Math*   © *Shell Education*

Regular Polygons

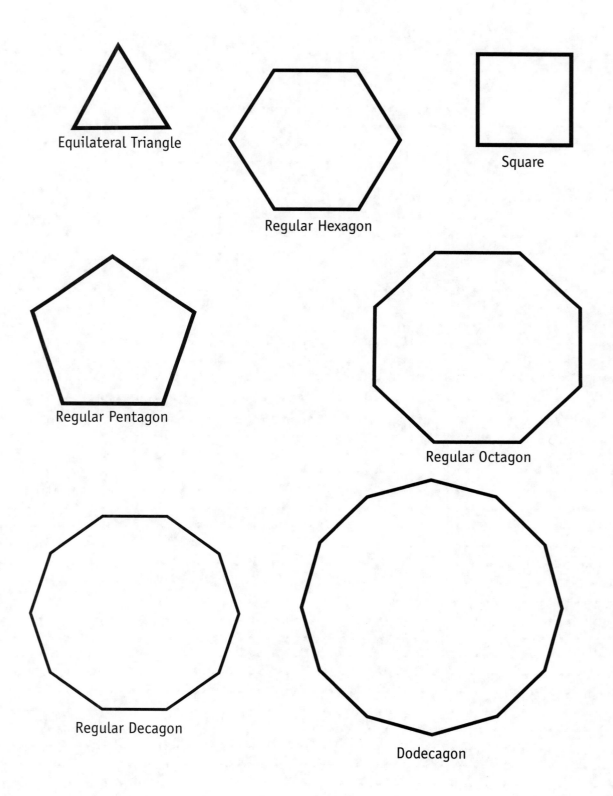

Equilateral Triangle

Regular Hexagon

Square

Regular Pentagon

Regular Octagon

Regular Decagon

Dodecagon

Templates & Manipulatives *(cont.)*

Dot Paper

#50026—*Graphing Calculator Strategies, Middle School Math*

Inch Rulers & Yard Stick

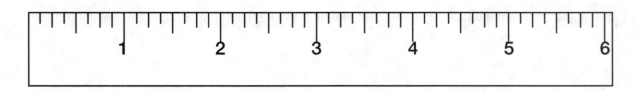

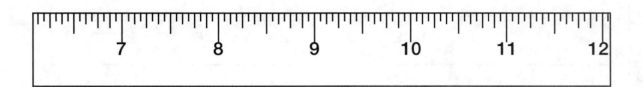

Templates & Manipulatives *(cont.)*

Centimeter Rulers

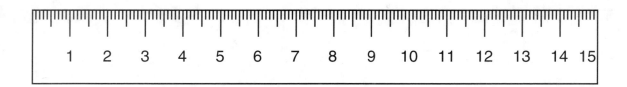

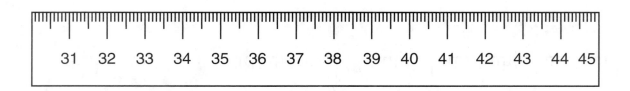

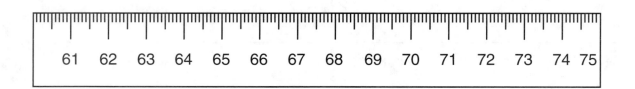

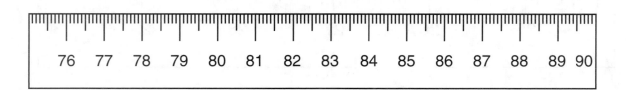

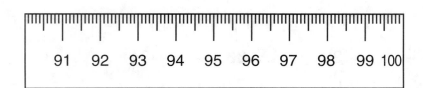

#50026—*Graphing Calculator Strategies, Middle School Math*

Glossary

algebraic expression—any term, or combination of terms, using variables that express an operation or series of operations

apps—the key that opens the menu of calculator software contained within the graphing calculator; each piece of software is also called an APP, short for application

area—the number of square units needed to cover a surface

arrow keys—sometimes called the cursor keys, these are the four keys on the upper right of the calculator that move the cursor in various calculator screens

clear—removal of either the last command line from the screen or the entire contents of the screen; it also refers to the button below the arrow keys

clrdraw—the command in the Draw menu that removes the contents from a graph screen

congruent—having the same size and shape; the symbol for congruence is $\cong$

coordinate plane—the plane determined by a horizontal number line, called the x-axis, and a vertical number line, called the y-axis; the x-axis and y-axis intersect at a point called the origin; an ordered pair (X, Y) of numbers represents each point in the coordinate plane

cube—a solid figure with six congruent square faces

cursor—the symbol displayed on the screen that indicates where the next keystroke will appear

customary system—system of measurement most commonly used in the United States

decagon—a polygon with 10 sides

decimal (decimal number)—a number with one or more digits to the right of the decimal

default—refers to the automatic settings of the calculator

delete—an action that removes a single character from the calculator screen; also refers to the calculator key that brings about this action

diameter—the length of a line segment whose endpoints are on a circle and which goes through the center

dodecagon—a polygon with 12 sides

edit—to write in data, particularly in a list; this is a menu choice on the Stat menu of the calculator

enter key— executes the existing command on the calculator screen, or in the case of applications, moves to a new screen or action for the application; the enter key is found in the lower right-hand corner of the calculator

equilateral triangle—a triangle with all sides of the same length

exponent—the number of times a term is multiplied by itself

fraction—a number that identifies part of a whole or part of a group

function—an expression given in the Y= screen of the calculator that represents a rule which gives *y*-values for the given *x*-values

graph—the key located in the upper–right section on the calculator that displays the graph screen

hexagon—a polygon with six sides and six angles

highlighted—the symbol or menu item that is currently selected; it is indicated by a darkened frame

home screen—the main screen of the calculator where calculations are displayed and various commands are carried out

hypotenuse—the side of a triangle opposite the right angle

integers—any whole numbers, the negative of these numbers, and zero

intersecting lines—a set of lines that meet or cross

leg—one of the two sides that form a right angle

length—a measured distance along a line or figure from one end to the other

line—straight path extending in both directions with no endpoints

linear equation—a first-degree equation with two variables whose graph is a straight line

list—a set of numerical data that has been entered into a list column, or displayed on the Home screen enclosed in brackets and separated by commas

manual fit—an item in the Stat/Calc menu that allows the user to create an estimated regression line for a scatter plot

mean—an average; the sum of a set of numbers divided by the number of members in the set

median—the middle number in a set of numbers that are in ascending order; if there is no single middle number, it is the mean of the two middle numbers

menu—a listing of choices that can be selected from a particular screen

metric system—a system of measurement based on tens and used globally

mode—in a list of data, it is the number that occurs most often

negative key—allows signed numbers to be created and is different from the subtraction key that refers to an operation

negative numbers—numbers less than zero

octagon —a polygon with eight sides

order of operations—rules describing what order to use when evaluating expressions; parentheses, exponents, multiply/divide, add/subtract

ordered pair—a pair of numbers that describes the location of a point on a grid, given in the following order: (horizontal coordinate, vertical coordinate) or (*x,y*)

parallel lines—lines that are always the same distance apart and that do not intersect; lines that have the same slope

parallelogram—a quadrilateral with opposite sides that are parallel and of equal length

pattern—a form or model by which elements can be arranged so that what comes next can be predicted

pentagon—a polygon with five sides

percent—a part of a whole expressed in hundredths

perimeter—the distance around a figure

point—an exact location in space that has no length, width, or thickness

polygon—a closed figure bounded by three or more straight sides

positive numbers—all numbers greater than zero

probability—measures how likely an event or outcome is

proportion—an equation that shows two equivalent ratios

quadrants—the four regions of a coordinate plane that are divided by the intersection of the *x*-axis and *y*-axis; numbered counterclockwise from the upper right, I, II, III, IV

quadrilateral—a four-sided polygon

quit—2nd of the Mode key, this is an action that returns from an existing screen to the Home screen. It is often used in applications to leave an active application or return to a previous screen

radius—the distance from the center to a point on the circle

range—difference between the greatest number and the least number in a set of data

ratio—a comparison of two measures or numbers by means of division

rectangle—a quadrilateral with two pairs of parallel sides and four right angles

rectangular prism—a prism with six rectangular faces

reflection—a transformation that involves a mirror image of a figure on the opposite side of a line

Glossary *(cont.)*

regular polygon—a polygon with angles the same measure and sides the same length

right angle—an angle that measures exactly 90 degrees

scale—a proportion between two sets of measurements

slope—the steepness of a line from left to right

square—a parallelogram with four equal sides and four right angles

square root—one of two identical factors

squared number—the product of two identical factors

standard window—the default window settings in which x's range from –10 to 10 with a scale of 1, y's do the same

stat—the key that accesses statistical commands and allows lists to be created and modified

stat plot—the 2nd of the Y= key that opens up settings for up to three plots of data

substitution—replacing a variable with a number

table—a column listing of x-values of a function and the corresponding y-values of the function

tessellation—a repeating pattern of shapes that fit together with no gaps and no overlaps

trace—the key next to the Graph key that allows points on a graph to be traced and coordinates to be displayed

trapezoid—a quadrilateral with one pair of parallel sides

triangle—a polygon with three angles and three sides

variable—a letter or symbol that stands for a number

volume—the number of cubic units it takes to fill a figure

width—horizontal measurements taken at the right angles to the length

***x*-axis**—the horizontal axis on a coordinate plane

***x*-coordinate**—the first value in the ordered pair that indicates the horizontal distance from the origin on a coordinate plane

***y*-axis**—the vertical axis on a coordinate plane

***y*-coordinate**—the second value in the ordered pair that indicates the vertical distance from the origin on a coordinate plane

***y*-intercept**—the point at which a line intersects the y-axis

Answer Key

Building Number Sense

Page 35
a. 4
b. 35
c. 0
d. –72
e. –1
f. 53
g. 42 + 12(2.5) = $72
h. 45 + 18(40) – 75 = $690

Page 36
a. –11/27
b. 1
c. 58/71
d. 49/11 = 4 5/11

Page 37
Answers will vary.

Page 42
a. 0.17
b. 1.77
c. 0.255
d. 0.03
e. 388.08
f. 1.32
g. 249.975
h. 388.5
i. 50.375
j. 484.96
k. 6.751
l. 137.34
m. 11.07
n. 1.76

Page 43

Fraction	Decimal	Percent
1/3	0.333	33 1/3%
2/3	0.667	66 2/3%
¼	0.25	25%
2/4	0.50	50%
¾	0.75	75%
1/5	0.20	20%
2/5	0.40	40%
3/5	0.60	60%
4/5	0.80	80%
1/6	0.167	16 2/3%
2/6	0.333	33 1/3%
3/6	0.50	50%
4/6	0.667	66 2/3%
5/6	0.833	83 1/3%
1/8	0.125	12.5%
2/8	0.25	25%
3/8	0.375	37.5%
4/8	0.50	50%
5/8	0.625	62.5%
6/8	0.75	75%
7/8	0.875	87.5%

Page 44
a. 81, C
b. 87, B
c. 85, B
d. 81, C

Page 45
Answers will vary.

Page 49
a. 840
b. 117
c. 52.5
d. 45.5
e. 24.75
f. 375
g. 275
h. 127.5
i. 129.25
j. 231

Building Number Sense *(cont.)*

Pages 50–51

	8 Servings		2 Servings	
Dec.	Dec.	Frac.	Dec.	Frac.
0.50	1.00	1/1	0.25	1/4
0.75	1.50	1 1/2	0.375	3/8
0.25	0.50	1/2	0.125	1/8
0.125	0.25	1/4	0.0625	1/16
2.00	4.00	4/1	1	1/1
0.375	0.75	3/4	0.1875	3/16
1.50	3.00	3/1	0.75	3/4
1.75	3.50	3 1/2	0.875	7/8
2.50	5.00	5/1	1.25	1 1/4
1.25	2.50	2 1/2	0.625	5/8
1.00	2.00	2/1	0.50	1/2

Page 52
a. 5
b. 6,734
c. 1 1/2 hours
d. **Sample 1:** 277.7 = 278
   Sample 2: 217.3 = 217
   Sample 3: 272.7 = 273
   Sample 4: 236.8 = 237
   Average or Estimate = 251

Page 53
1–7. *Answers included in the activity.*
8–10. *Answers may vary.*

Page 60
a. 5
b. 4
c. −2
d. −5
e. −3
f. −4
g. −6
h. −12
i. 18
j. −72
k. 6

Page 60 *(cont.)*
l. −3
m. −20
n. 24
o. −3
p. −6
q.

Positive or Negative	Problem	Answer
negative	−5(−4)(−3) =	−60
positive	−2(−4)(−6)(−6) =	288
negative	−9(−2)(−7) =	−126
positive	−3(−5)(−9)(−7) =	945

r. negative
s. positive

Pages 61–62

a.
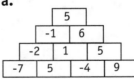

b.

c.

d.

e.
$7 - 4 - 2 + 8 = 9$

f.
$5 - 12 - 3 + 18 - 10 = -2$

g.
negative; -243

h.
positive; 6,561

i.

−256	2	−64
8	32	128
−16	512	−4

j.

−2	−9	12
−36	6	−1
3	−4	−18

k. *Answers may vary.*

Page 63
Answers may vary.

Thinking Algebraically

Page 71

Row (*x*)	Number of Squares (*y*)
1	3
2	5
3	7
4	9
nth	$2x + 1$

a. 2
b. 13
c. $2x + 1$
d. $2x + 1$
e. 1 horizontal unit; 2 vertical units
f. 2; (0, 1)

Row (*x*)	Number of Squares (*y*)
1	1
2	2
3	3
4	4
nth	x

g. 1
h. 6
i. x
j. x
k. 1 horizontal unit; 1 vertical unit
l. 1; (0, 0)

Page 72

Figure (*x*)	Number of Squares (*y*)
1	5
2	8
3	11
nth	$3X + 2$

a. 3
b. 20
c. $3x + 2$
d. $3x + 2$
e. 3 vertical units; 1 horizontal unit
f. 3; (0, 2)
g. -1; -3; $2x - 1$
h. -1; -4; $3x - 1$

Page 73

I.
  a. 4
  b. (0, 1)
  c. $y = 4x + 1$
II.
  d. 2
  e. (0, −2)
  f. $2x − 2$
III.
  g. 3
  h. (0, 4)
  i. $y = 3x + 4$
IV.
  j. −2
  k. (0, 3)
  l. $y = −2x + 3$

Page 77

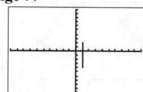

a. Vertical
b. $x = 1$

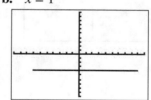

c. Horizontal
d. $y = −4$

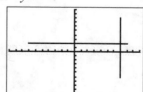

e. Vertical
f. $x = 7$
g. Horizontal
h. $y = 2$
i. (7, 2)

Thinking Algebraically *(cont.)*

Page 78

  a. *Answers will vary.*
  b. $(-3, -6)$
  c. *Graphs may vary.*
  d. *Answers will vary.*
  e. $(5, -2)$
  f. *Graphs may vary.*
  g. *Answers will vary.*
  h. $(-7, 4)$
  i. *Graphs may vary.*

Page 79

  a.

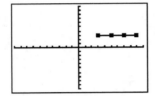

x	y
3	3
5	3
7	3
9	3

  b. Horizontal
  c. $y = 3$
  d.

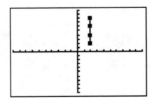

x	y
2	2
2	4
2	6
2	8

  e. Vertical
  f. $x = 2$
g–h. Answers will vary.
  i. $y = 7$
  j. $x = 4$
  k. $(4, 7)$

Page 84

  a. $1.290322581 = 1.29$
  b. $1332.031 = 1332.03$
  c. -116.25
  d. $8.744 = 8.74$
e–f. *Answers will vary.*
  g. $1.675 = 1.68$
  h. $.125 = 0.13$
  i. $0.825 = 0.83$
  j. 0.75
k–l. *Answers will vary.*
  m. $33.30; Multiply $37 by 0.10, which equals $3.70. Then subtract $3.70 from $37.00, which equals $33.30
  n. Multiply the cost of the shoe by the percentage of the cost paid, e.g. $37 x 90%.
  o. 90%; You get the sale price.

Page 85

a–b. *Answers will vary.*

Page 86

a–g. *Answers will vary.*

Page 91

  a. $(-4, -4)$
  b. $(4, -1)$

$y = 5x + 3$		$y = 3x + 7$	
x	y	x	y
−1	−2	−1	4
0	3	0	7
1	8	1	10
2	13	2	13

  c. $(2, 13)$
  d. Rose: $y = 4x + 8$; Rick: $y = 5x + 5$; x = miles; y = total miles
  e. Mile marker 20 (Hint: Create a ZoomFit window.)

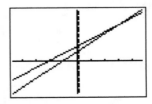

Answer Key *(cont.)*

Thinking Algebraically *(cont.)*

Page 92

a. Greg: $y = 0.35x + 8.25$; Frank: $y = 0.25x + 9.55$
x = days; y = total allowance

b. On the 13th day

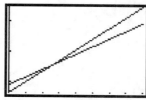

Hint: Use a ZoomFit window.

c. Rental A: $y = 0.55x + 55.50$;
Rental B: $y = 0.35x + 66.50$
x = miles; y = total cost

d. 55 miles;

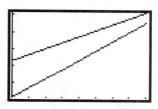

Hint: Use a ZoomFit window.

e. Rental A for 49, Rental B for 68

Analyzing Data

Page 99

a.

tens	ones
0	6, 9, 9
1	1, 1, 1, 2, 2, 3, 4, 5, 5, 5, 6, 8, 8, 9
2	0, 0, 5

b. Mean: 14.45; Median: 14.5; Mode: 11, 15;
Range: 19

c. $350 – $289 = $61; Based on the average
($14.45) it will take about 5 or more days.

d.

dollars	cents
0	25, 25, 30, 30, 35, 45, 45, 50, 75, 75, 75
1	00, 50, 50

e. Mean: $0.65; Median: $0.48; Mode: $0.75,
Range: $1.25

f. *Answers will vary.*

g.

tens	ones
7	8, 9
8	3, 3, 5, 5, 6, 6, 7, 8

h. Mean: 84; Median: 85; Mode: 83, 85, 86;
Range: 10

Page 100

a.

stem	leaf
38	127, 902
40	800
42	000, 059, 445, 531
43	000, 500
48	500
50	062, 345, 381
55	777
56	000, 500

b. Mean: 46,308.0625; Median: 43,250; Mode:
None; Range: 18,373

c. Answers will vary.

Page 101–102

a–l. Answers will vary.

Page 107

a. Heads: 1/2; Tails: 1/2

b–c. *Answers will vary.*

d. (1) 1/6; (2) 1/6; (3) 1/6; (4) 1/6; (5) 1/6; (6) 1/6

e–f. *Answers will vary.*

g. (1) 1/4; (2) 1/4; (3) 1/4; (4) 1/4

h–j. *Answers will vary.*

Pages 108–109

a. Booths 1 and 3

b. Booths 4 and 5

c–g. *Answers will vary.*

Page 110

a. (1) 1/4; (2) 1/4; (3) 1/4; (4) 1/4

b–e. *Answers will vary.*

Page 114

a.

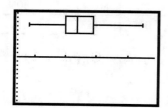

Answer Key *(cont.)*

Analyzing Data *(cont.)*

Page 114 *(cont.)*

b. Mean: 4.385; Median: 4.35; Upper Quartile: 4.9; Lower Quartile: 4; Upper Extreme: 6.5; Lower Extreme: 2.8

c.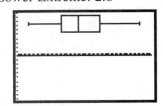

d. Mean: 45.675; Median: 45; Upper Quartile: 55.5; Lower Quartile: 37; Upper Extreme: 75; Lower Extreme: 21

e. *Answers will vary.*

Pages 115–116

Answers will vary.

Pages 117-118

a.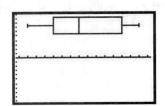

b. Mean: 23.736; Median: 23; Upper Quartile: 28; Lower Quartile: 20; Upper Extreme: 30; Lower Extreme: 17

c–d. *Answers will vary.*

Pages 123–124

a.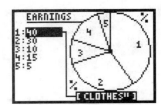

b.

Category	$/month	Frac.	Dec.	%
Clothes	$16.00	2/5	.40	40%
Music	$6.00	3/20	.15	15%
Movies	$4.00	1/10	.10	10%
Savings	$12.00	3/10	.30	30%
Misc.	$2.00	1/20	.05	5%

c. Clothes: $80; Music: $30; Movies: $20; Savings $60; Misc: $10

Pages 123–124 *(cont.)*

d. Percents: Baseball = 18.42%, Gymnastics = 2.63%, Tennis = 7.89%, Soccer = 31.58%, Swimming = 13.16%, Basketball = 26.32%

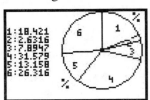

e.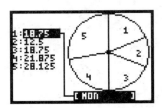

f. Students: Mon. = 60, Tues. = 40, Wed. = 60, Thurs. = 70, Fri. = 90

Page 125

a–c. *Answers will vary.*

Page 126

a–g. *Answers will vary.*

Developing Spatial Reasoning

Page 132

I.

a.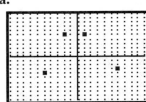

b.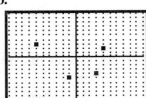

II. (4, –1), (2, –6), (–5, –3)

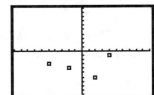

III.

c. Area = 30 square units

III.

d. Perimeter = 22 units

Answer Key *(cont.)*

Developing Spatial Reasoning *(cont.)*
Page 133

a. 50 units²; 30 units

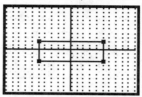

b. 28 units²; 25.6 units

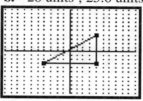

Page 133 *(cont.)*

c. 32 units²; 27.4 units

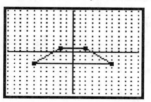

d. 100 units²; 40 units

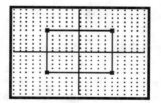

Page 134

I.

l1	l2
–4	3
4	3
4	–3
–1	1
0	0
6	1
–4	–3
–1	–5
5	–5

II–III. *Answers will vary.*
Page 139

a.

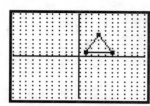

b.

x	y
–4	4
0	4
–2	8
–4	4

c.

x	y
4	–3
8	–3
6	1
4	–3

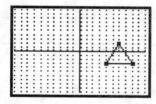

d.

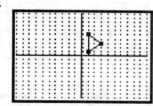

e.

x	y
1	–1
3	–3
1	–5
1	–1

f.

x	y
–1	1
–3	3
–1	5
–1	1

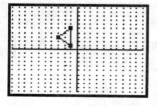

Page 140
a–f. *Answers will vary.*

Developing Spatial Reasoning *(cont.)*

Page 141

1–7 *Answers will vary.*

Pages 145–146

  a. 1573.1 cm^3
  b. 4965.2 ft^3
  c. 828.4 mm^3
  d. 11015.1 in^3
  e.

	Length	Width	Height
Cube	4	4	4
Rectangular Prism	*Answers will vary.*	*Answers will vary.*	*Answers will vary.*
Rectangular Prism	*Answers will vary.*	*Answers will vary.*	*Answers will vary.*

  f.

	Length	Width	Height
Cube	6	6	6
Rectangular Prism	*Answers will vary.*	*Answers will vary.*	*Answers will vary.*
Rectangular Prism	*Answers will vary.*	*Answers will vary.*	*Answers will vary.*

  g.

	Length	Width	Height
Cube	9	9	9
Rectangular Prism	*Answers will vary.*	*Answers will vary.*	*Answers will vary.*
Rectangular Prism	*Answers will vary.*	*Answers will vary.*	*Answers will vary.*

  h.

	Length	Width	Height
Cube	12	12	12
Rectangular Prism	*Answers will vary.*	*Answers will vary.*	*Answers will vary.*
Rectangular Prism	*Answers will vary.*	*Answers will vary.*	*Answers will vary.*

Page 147

  a. optimal box depth: 2.326 inches, length 6.347, width 3.847 inches
  b–k. *Answers will vary.*

Page 148

Length	Vol.	3	2	1	None
2	8	8	0	0	0
3	27	8	12	6	1
4	64	8	24	24	8
5	125	8	36	54	27
6	216	8	48	96	64
n	n^3	8	$12(n-2)$	$6(n-2)^2$	$(n-2)^3$

  a. Volume: n^3; 3 Faces: stays at 8; 2 faces: $12(n-2)$; 1 face: $6(n-2)^2$; 0 faces $(n-2)^3$
  b. 8000 units^3
  c. 8; 216; 1944; 5832
  d. 32768 units^3
  e. 8; 360; 5,400; 27,000
  f. 166375 units^3
  g. 8; 636; 16854; 148877

Page 153

  a. *Answers will vary.*
  b. *Predictions will vary.* Equilateral triangles, quadrilaterals, and hexagons will tessellate.
  c. *Predictions will vary.* A regular polygon will tessellate if the vertex angle is a divisor of 360°.
  d. $(n-2)180/n$, where n = number of sides
  e.

Shape	Number of Sides	Vertex Angle	Divisor of 360°
Equilateral Triangle	3	60	Yes
Square	4	90	Yes
Pentagon	5	108	No
Hexagon	6	120	Yes
Octagon	8	135	No
Decagon	10	144	No
Dodecagon	12	150	No

Pages 154–155

1–4. *Answers will vary.*
a–c. *Answers will vary.*

Answer Key *(cont.)*

Appendix E

Working with Units of Measurements
Page 163

a.

Triangle	Area of a	Area of b	Area of c
1 Right	9	16	25
2 Right	25	144	169
3 Right	49	576	625

b. Sum of the areas of *a* and *b* equal the area of *c*.
c. Squaring the side
d.

	Triangle	Length *a*	Length *b*	Length *c*
1	Right	3^2	4^2	5^2
2	Right	5^2	12^2	13^2
3	Right	7^2	24^2	25^2

e. $a^2 + b^2 = c^2$
f. $c = 8.6$ cm
g. $b = 8.3$ in.

Page 164
a. 2.8 cm
b. 3.8 yd.
c. 6.4 in.
d. 44.1 m
e. 5.5 ft.
f. 6.8 mm
g. 10.9 ft.
h. 127.3 ft.

Page 165
a. $c = 29.8$ in.
b. 16.2 in.; No
c. 12 cm
d. $c = 12.2$ miles
e. $a = 3.1$ ft.
f.

# of Odd #'s	Sum
1	1
2	4
3	9
4	16
5	25
6	36
n	n^2
50	2500

Page 166
a. $a = 38.5$ square units; $p = 31.0$ units
b. $a = 45$ square units; $p = 32.5$ units
c. $a = 70$ square units; $p = 34.6$ units
d. $a = 90$ square units; $p = 39.0$ units

Page 170
a. Rectangle = length x width; Square = side^2;
   Parallelogram = height x base;
   Triangle = 1/2 height x base
   Trapezoid = 1/2 (base1 + base2) x height
   Circle = πr^2
b. $a = 194$ cm^2; $p = 56.9$ cm
c. $a = 2.9$ in.^{2}; $p = 6.8$ in.
d. $a = 30$ ft.^{2}; $p = 22.8$ ft.
e. $a = 24$ mm^2; $p = 24$ mm
f. $a = 50$ yd^2; $p = 31.6$ yd
g. $a = 98.5$ cm^2; $c = 35.2$ cm
h. $s = 15.5$ ft. x 15.5 ft.
i. *Answers will vary.*

Page 171
a. $a = 38$ square units; $p = 30$ units
b. $a = 42$ square units; $p = 34.83$ units
c. $a = 49$ square units; $p = 36.47$ units
d. $a = 84$ square units; $p = 45.21$ units
e. *Answers will vary, may include dividing the shapes into regular polygons.*

Page 172

Room	Area
Bedroom 1	64 ft^2
Bedroom 2	112 ft^2
Bedroom 3	144 ft^2
Bathroom	64 ft^2
Mstr. Bedroom	244 ft^2
Mstr. Bathroom	64 ft^2
Living Room	420 ft^2
Kitchen	288 ft^2
Dining Room	96 ft^2
Foyer	24 ft^2
Hallway	80 ft^2
Total Area	1600 ft^2

Page 173
Answers will vary.

© Shell Education   #50026—Graphing Calculator Strategies, Middle School Math   223

Working with Units of Measurements *(cont.)*
Page 180

a.

L3 (x)	L4 (y)
4	4
−4	4
−4	−4
4	−4
4	4

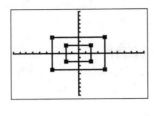

b. Square
c. Length: 12 units; Width: 12 units; Area: 144 square units; Perimeter: 48 units

d.

L3 (x)	L4 (y)
−8	2
−8	−6
2	−6
2	2
−8	2

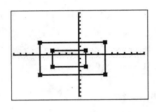

e. Rectangle
f. 13.75 units by 11 units; 151.25 units^2; 49.5 units

g.

L3 (x)	L4 (y)
−4	3
−4	−3
4	−3
4	3
−4	3

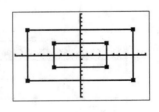

h. Rectangle
i. Length: 4 units; Width: 3 units; Area: 12 square units; Perimeter: 14 units
j. *Answers will vary.*
k. *Answers will vary.*

Page 182
a–h. *Answers will vary.*

Page 183
a–f. *Answers will vary.*

Pages 190–191
a–c. *Answers will vary.*

Page 192
  a. 36 in; 91.44 cm
  b. 600 cm; 19.68 ft.
  c. 32 pints; 15.14 L
  d. 1.637 L; 3.45 pints
  e. 413000 g; 910.5 lbs.
  f. 3.46 kg; 7.65 lbs.
  g. 147.4 kg
  h. 160 lbs.
  i. Shaquille: 147, 418 g; Venus: 72,600 g
  j. 2.16 m
  k. 5 ft. 11 in.
  l. Shaquille: 85 in; Venus: 71 in.
 m. Shaquile: 216 cm; Venus: 180 cm
  n. 165 lbs; 74.8 kg
  o. 14 in; 36 cm

Page 193
a–f. *Answers will vary.*